C000082700

1 MONTH OF
FREE
READING

at

www.ForgottenBooks.com

By purchasing this book you are eligible for one month membership to ForgottenBooks.com, giving you unlimited access to our entire collection of over 1,000,000 titles via our web site and mobile apps.

To claim your free month visit:
www.forgottenbooks.com/free920511

* Offer is valid for 45 days from date of purchase. Terms and conditions apply.

ISBN 978-0-266-99433-6
PIBN 10920511

This book is a reproduction of an important historical work. Forgotten Books uses
state-of-the-art technology to digitally reconstruct the work, preserving the original format
whilst repairing imperfections present in the aged copy. In rare cases, an imperfection in
the original, such as a blemish or missing page, may be replicated in our edition. We do,
however, repair the vast majority of imperfections successfully; any imperfections that
remain are intentionally left to preserve the state of such historical works.

Forgotten Books is a registered trademark of FB &c Ltd.
Copyright © 2018 FB &c Ltd.
FB &c Ltd, Dalton House, 60 Windsor Avenue, London, SW19 2RR.
Company number 08720141. Registered in England and Wales.

For support please visit www.forgottenbooks.com

A CATECHISM OF CATHOLIC EDUCATION

BY

REVEREND JAMES H. RYAN, D.D., PH.D.

Executive Secretary, Department of Education, N. C. W. C.

NATIONAL CATHOLIC WELFARE COUNCIL

BUREAU OF EDUCATION

WASHINGTON, D. C.

1922

𝔑ibil 𝔒bstat:

LUDOVICUS R. S

Censo

𝔦mprimatur:

✠ MICHAEL J.
Archiepiscopus B

die 27, Februarii, 1922.

Copyright, 1922,

by

NATIONAL CATHOLIC WELFARE COUN(

MAR 16 1922

©CLA654939

The Paulist Press, New York, N. Y.

TABLE OF CONTENTS

INTRODUCTION

THE Catholic school is one of the greatest moral facts in the United States. During 1920, 1,981,051 children were educated in Catholic schools. The Catholic school system is an institution of which every Catholic has good reasons to be proud. Its teachers are men and women well trained for their tasks. The quality of the work accomplished is of an exceptionally high order. Its Americanism is beyond question. To inform further our Catholic people on the history, administration and organization of their schools is the aim of this Catechism of Catholic Education.

This Catechism may be made the subject of study in the home and in the school. Clubs and organizations of men and women will find it a convenient manual for an elementary study of Catholic education in all its phases.

One of the primary functions of the Department of Education of the National Catholic Welfare Council is to spread information concerning Catholic education. The Department stands ready at all times to assist schools, clubs and organizations in the formation of groups for the study of what the Catholic school is and what it is accomplishing.

CHAPTER I

HISTORY OF CATHOLIC EDUCATION IN THE UNITED STATES

1. Q. When were Catholic schools first established in the United States?

A. The first Catholic schools were established in what are now the States of Florida and New Mexico. Most of these schools were founded for the education of the Indians. As early as 1606, however, a classical school had been established in St. Augustine, Florida.

By 1629, four years before the foundation of the first school in the thirteen original Colonies, there were many elementary schools in New Mexico. Most of these schools were destroyed in 1680. The Spanish colonists were obliged by law to found schools in every village where they settled.

There were also many pre-Revolutionary schools in Texas and California, due to the zeal of Jesuit and Franciscan missionaries. These schools were largely industrial schools.

2. Q. When and from what country did the first body of Catholic teachers come?

A. The first group of elementary school teachers to come to the United States were ten Ursuline Sisters from France, who, in 1727, founded in New Orleans the first Catholic academy and day school for girls in the New World.

3. Q. Had Catholic schools been established in other places prior to 1776?

A. Before 1776 schools had been established in St. Louis, Detroit, Kaskaskia, as well as in what are now the States of Maine, Maryland, New York and Pennsylvania.

4. Q. At what date was the first Catholic college established in the United States?

A. The first Catholic college was opened in 1677 at Newtown, Maryland, by the Society of Jesus.

Georgetown College, the direct descendant of schools established at Newtown and Bohemia, dates from 1789.

5. Q. What was the number of Catholic schools in the United States prior to 1776?

A. Upwards of 70 Catholic schools existed within the present confines of the United States. Considering the social and economic conditions prevailing amongst the small number of Catholics in pre-Revolutionary days, this is quite remarkable. The total Catholic population in 1789 amounted only to 35,000.

6. Q. Were the Colonial schools State or religious schools?

A. All the schools in the Colonies, whether established by Catholics or Protestants, were religious schools. There were no State schools, supported solely by public taxation.

7. Q. What was the necessary consequence of this fact?

A. The fact that all religious denominations maintained schools resulted in Catholic settlers organizing and developing a school system of their own.

8. Q. What was the general character of the Catholic schools of the Colonial period?

A. Catholic Colonial schools were modeled either after Continental schools, especially French and German, or after the system of education established by the Jesuits.

The curriculum was elementary, consisting mainly of reading, writing and arithmetic.

9. Q. Were the Catholic schools of Colonial days merely separate schools or did they form a system?

A. The elements of a system existed even in Colonial days, as all the schools in the English Colonies were under the direction of the Jesuits.

10. Q. What principal factors determined the growth of Catholic schools in the United States after the year 1800?

A. The most important factors were: ·

(1) The creation and introduction of religious teaching communities into the country;

(2) The expansion of the Church;

(3) Financial assistance from Europe.

11. Q. How did the creation and introduction of religious teaching communities assist in the development of Catholic education?

A. By supplying the demand for teachers of the numerous schools, which grew up so rapidly all over the country.

The Poor Clares in 1799 founded a school at Georgetown. This school was afterwards continued by the Sisters of the Visitation. The community of the Visitation Sisters, together with the Sisters of Charity (the first American religious teaching order), the Sisters of Loretto, the Sisters of Charity of Nazareth and the Sisters of St. Dominic grew amazingly, and in the period between 1800-50 supplied the great majority of teachers for our Catholic schools.

As each one of these orders maintained a training school for its teachers, the quality of the work accomplished by them in the numerous academies and parish schools under their direction was of a very high order.

12. Q. How did the growth of the Church affect the development of Catholic education?

A. The expansion of the Church, following on the division of the country into dioceses and archdioceses, created new demands for educational institutions. In 1829, a provincial council held in Baltimore ordered the establishment of Catholic schools "wherever possible." The decree of the Council put the seal of ecclesiastical approval on the rapidly developing Catholic school system.

13. Q. How did financial assistance from Europe aid in the development of Catholic education?

A. Financial assistance from Europe, especially from France and Austria, greatly aided the struggling Catholic schools in their development. Most of the early Catholic settlers were poor, and, unassisted, they could not have carried the financial burden of building schools and churches. The numerous contributions which came from Europe supplemented gifts of the laity in this country and made possible the erection of many schools which, otherwise, could not have been built.

14. Q. What factors influenced the development of the Catholic school system after 1850?

A. (a) One of the principal factors was the controversy over the appropriation of State funds to sectarian schools. Bishop John Hughes of New York presented the Catholic plea for a just share of the public school fund. His plea was rejected. It became evident to all that in the future Catholics would have to maintain their schools without financial assistance from the State.

At this time the public school system, tax-supported, became a reality. Most of the Protestant denominations that conducted schools fought vigorously the principle of public education. They were defeated. The public schools of that period were practically Protestant schools and bitterly anti-Catholic. Most of the teachers were Protestants. The Protestant Bible was read in the public school. A spirit of antagonism to Catholic principles remained a characteristic of the public school system in many places until quite recently. Catholics could not in conscience, therefore, send their children to such schools; the only alternative was to establish schools of their own and to perpetuate those which already existed.

(b) The great number of immigrants to the United States at this time, especially from Ireland and Germany, doubled the Catholic population and made necessary a wide extension of the Catholic school system. Religious teachers followed in the wake of the immigrants, and through the zeal and sacrifice of both, the secure foundations of the present-day Catholic school system were laid. Not only were parish schools erected alongside of our churches, but high schools, seminaries and colleges grew in numbers.

(c) Ecclesiastical legislation made secure the position of the Catholic school as a necessary adjunct to the Church. Church authorities ordered the establishment of Catholic schools "in every place," and the Third Council of Baltimore (1884) enacted school legislation which has, since that time been the basis and the norm of the development of the Catholic school system.

15. Q. What has been the development of Catholic schools from 1870 to the present day?

A. The Civil War retarded the growth of Catholic schools for a time. After 1875, however, they increased in number and in attendance with surprising rapidity. The growth of Catholic education since 1875 has been a normal, steady one as the following tables show:

TABLE SHOWING GROWTH OF PARISH SCHOOL ATTENDANCE
FROM 188 TO 1920.

Year	Attendance	Periodical Increase	Percentage of Periodical Increase	Total Increase	Percentage of Total Increase
1880......	405,234	....	...	....	....
1885......	490,531	85,297	21.04	85,297	21.04
1890......	633,238	142,707	29.62	228,004	56.64
1895......	755,038	121,800	19.23	349,804	86.35
1 90......	854,523	99,485	13.17	449,289	110.87
1905......	1,031,378	176,855	20.69	626,144	154.88
1910......	1,237,251	205873	19.96	832,017	205.31
1915......	1,456,200	218,955	17.69	1,050,972	259.34
1920......	1,795,673	339,467	23.31	1,390,439	343.12

Figures taken from the *Official Catholic Directory*. For 1920 the figures are from *Directory of Catholic Colleges and Schools.*

TABLE SHOWING GROWTH OF ATTENDANCE AT SEMINARIES FOR THE EDUCATION OF CANDIDATES FOR THE PRIESTHOOD FROM 1880 TO 1920.

Year	Attendance	Periodical Increase	Percentage of Periodical Increase	Total Increase	Percentage of Total Increase
1880	1,136	....	....	....	....
1885	1,597	461	40.6	461	40.6
1890	2,132	535	33.5	996	87.7
1895	2,353	221	10.4	1,217	107.1
1900	1,998	....	....	....	....
1905	3,926	1,928	96.5	2,790	245.6
1910	6,182	2,256	57.5	5,046	444.2
1915	6,770	558	9.5	5,634	495.9
1920	11,198	4,428	65.5	10,062	885.7

Figures taken from *Official Catholic Directory.* For 1920 the figures are from *Directory of Catholic Colleges and Schools.*

NOTE—The number of seminaries has increased from 24 in 1880 to 164 in 1920. The 1920 total (164) includes 113 seminaries for the education of the religious clergy and 51 for the education of the diocesan clergy. Students who reside outside the United States are not included in the above.

● References

Burns, *Principles, Or   and Establishment of the Catholic School System in the United States,* Benziger, N. Y., 1912.

Burns, *Growth and Development of the Catholic School System in the United States,* Benziger, N. Y., 1912.

Cubberley, *Public Education in the United States,* Houghton Mifflin & Company, Boston, 1919.

McCormick, *History of Education,* Catholic Education Press, Washington, 1912.

Pace, "Catholic Education," in *Catholic Encyclopedia,* Encyclopedia Press, N. Y., 1910.

Official Catholic Directory for 1880, 1885, 1890, 1895, 1900, 1905, 1910 and 1915.

Ryan, *Directory of Catholic Colleges and Schools,* Bureau of Education, N. C. W. C., Washington, 1921.

CHAPTER II

STATISTICS OF CATHOLIC EDUCATION IN THE UNITED STATES

CATHOLIC SCHOOL CENSUS, 1920

1. Q. How many Catholic schools are there in the United States?

A. 8,706, including all kinds.

2. Q. How many teachers are there in the Catholic schools of the United States?

A. 54,265 teachers are engaged in the 8,706 Catholic schools.

3. Q. Are all the teachers in Catholic schools priests or members of religious orders?

A. No. 1,929 lay professors teach in Catholic universities and colleges; 953 in Catholic high schools, and 2,989 in Catholic elementary schools.

4. Q. How many students attend the Catholic schools?

A. 1,981,051.

5. Q. How many Catholic elementary schools are there in the United States?

A. There are 6,551, including 358 institutional schools. 41,581 teachers are employed in these schools. 1,795,673 boys and girls attend the Catholic elementary schools.

6. Q. How many Catholic high schools are there?

A. There are 1,552 Catholic high schools, 7,924 high school teachers, and 129,838 high school students.

7. Q. How many religious novitiates and normal training schools are there?

A. 309, with an attendance of 10,544.

8. Q. How many Catholic colleges are there?

A. There are 114 Catholic colleges, 62 for men and 52 for women. They employ 1,697 professors and have an attendance of 13,996. Of this number, 8,343 are men and 5,653 women.

9. Q. How many seminaries are there?

A. 164 seminaries with 1,063 professors and 11,198 students for the priesthood.

10. Q. How many Catholic universities are there in the United States?

A. There are 16 Catholic universities with a teaching staff of 2,000 and an attendance of 19,803.

NATIONAL SUMMARY OF CATHOLIC SCHOOL STATISTICS

Schools	Number	Professors	Teachers	Students
Universities	16	2,000		19,802
Colleges	114	1,697		13,996
Seminaries	164	1,063		11,198
High Schools	1,552		7,924	129,838
Normal Training Schools	309	*	*	10,544
Elementary Schools	6,551		41,581	1,795,673
Total	8,706	4,760	49,505	1,981,051

The above statistics are based on returns made to inquiries sent out by the Department of Education, N. C. W. C., and published in the *Directory of Catholic Colleges and Schools.*

*No Exact Data Available.

REFERENCES

Ryan, *Directory of Catholic Colleges and Schools,* Bureau of Education, N. C. W. C., Washington, 1921.

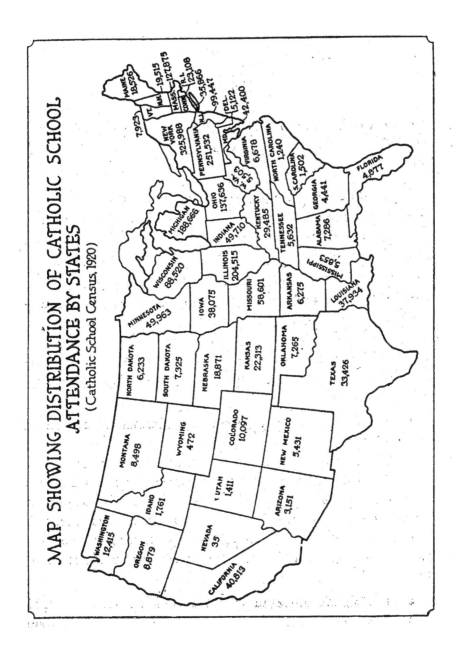

MAP SHOWING DISTRIBUTION OF CATHOLIC SCHOOL ATTENDANCE BY STATES

(Catholic School Census, 1920)

CHAPTER III

Organization of the Catholic School System

1. Q. How are Catholic schools organized?

A. Catholic schools are organized on the diocesan plan, each diocese forming a separate unit. In each diocese the bishop is *ex officio* head of school administration.

2. Q. If the bishop is the head of the diocesan school system, is not then each diocese independent in the administration of its educational affairs?

A. Yes; each diocese like each State is autonomous in education, formulating its own laws, devising its own policies, and administering its own district without external interference.

3. Q. Does the bishop personally administer the school system?

A. Under the bishop as chairman there is usually a school board, commission or committee which establishes standards, inspects schools, approves text-books—in a word, performs all the functions of a State Department of Education. Practically all matters pertaining to elementary education in a diocese are under the jurisdiction of this board.

4. Q. Has the diocesan school system an official agent?

A. Yes; the official agent of the diocesan school system is the diocesan superintendent or supervisor of schools, who

12

is generally a member of the diocesan board of education and is appointed by the bishop.

5. Q. What are the duties of a diocesan superintendent or supervisor of schools?

A. The diocesan superintendent represents the bishop in the government of the schools. He acts also as the executive officer of the school board in carrying out programs and policies for the development of the schools under his jurisdiction. He therefore inspects schools, holds examinations for pupils, makes provision for the professional growth of the teaching force and organizes the educational resources of his diocese.

The diocesan superintendent publishes a yearly report, giving a complete statistical account of the schools over which he has charge and submits recommendations for the improvement of the same. The diocesan superintendent of schools occupies much the same position as a State Superintendent of Public Instruction in the public school system.

6. Q. What are community supervisors?

A. Community supervisors or inspectors are members of religious teaching orders, who inquire into the work of the teachers belonging to their own order and report on it, to their immediate religious superiors. They are not diocesan school officials and therefore have no official status. In some dioceses, however, they are appointed by the bishop.

7. Q. What are the reasons for the existence of community supervisors?

A. Since the majority of teachers in our Catholic schools are members of religious communities, it is to the interest of each community to inspect the work of its own members. The supervision which these community supervisors exert over their own teachers results in inestimable good to the

TABLE SHOWING FUNCTIONS OF DIOCESAN SUPERVISOR OF SCHOOLS FOR ARCHDIOCESE OF BOSTON.

ARCHDIOCESE OF BOSTON SUPERVISION OF PARISH SCHOOLS.

ARCHBISHOP OF BOSTON,

DIOCESAN SUPERVISOR OF SCHOOLS.

INTER-ORGANIZATION RELATIONS			EXTRA ORGANIZATION RELATIONS	
	RELIGIOUS COMMUNITIES			
Schools	Board of Community Supervisors	Principals and Teachers	Educational	General
1. Visitation of Academies Parish Schools Institutional Schools	1. Advisory in matters of policy.	1. Conferences for Principals and Teachers.	1. Study of Educational Legislation.	1. Bureau of Information and Statistics.
2. Uniform Regulations Curriculum Tests Reports Annual Monthly	2. Supervision of teaching force.	2. Diocesan Institute and professional ones for teachers.	2. Contact with Public School Officials.	2. Lectures and addresses.
			3. Lectures at Novitiate Normal Schools and Diocesan Seminary.	3. Annual Report and Articles for Press.

teachers, the schools, and the diocese. These supervisors are also of great assistance to the diocesan superintendent of schools, helping him to keep in close contact with the different teaching communities and offering him a splendid means of putting into effect the regulations and recommendations of the diocesan school board.

8. Q. What are school principals?

A. A school principal is the head of a single elementary or parish school. He is usually a member of the religious order which supplies the teaching staff of the school.

9. Q. What are the duties of a school principal?

A. He has immediate and personal charge of the school and works under the direction of the pastor. Both the work of the principal and that of the teachers under his care are supervised by the diocesan superintendent of schools.

10. Q. How are institutional schools administered?

A. Institutional schools are directed by the Diocesan Supervisor of Charities. Many progressive educators, however, are of the opinion that these schools should become an integral part of the Diocesan School System, and that the educational training given in the same should be under the supervision of the Diocesan Superintendent of Schools.

11. Q. How are Catholic high schools organized?

A. (a) In some dioceses a high school board similar in make-up to the diocesan school board has control of all high schools. The active agent of this board is the diocesan superintendent of high schools. This plan has worked well wherever it has been tried out. Many dioceses are preparing to adopt it.

(b) In dioceses where there is no high school board, the high schools are administered either by principals appointed by the bishop (if the institution is diocesan) or by principals selected by the religious community which controls the school.

12. Q. How are colleges and universities administered?
A. By a president and board of trustees.

If the college or university is a diocesan institution, the bishop is ordinarily chancellor of the same or chairman of its board of directors. If the college or university, however, is maintained by a religious order or community, its administrative and educational policies are immediately under the direction of the religious superior or provincial of the order concerned.

Seminaries for the education of candidates for the diocesan priesthood are usually under the supervision of the bishop in whose diocese they are located. Seminaries for religious are administered in much the same way as colleges and universities.

13. Q. What are some features of Catholic school organization?
A. The following features are most noteworthy: Freedom, cohesion, and unity.

(a) There is no superdiocesan or supernational organization which dictates to the Catholic schools what they must do. Curriculum, training of teachers, and standards of instruction are developed and maintained as the needs of each diocese require. Educational theories and fads cannot be imposed on a diocesan system from without. The diocese, however, is free to accept any tried methods of instruction or administration which in its judgment meets its own needs. Home rule in education is one of the significant characteristics of the diocesan school system.

(b) As our schools are under episcopal jurisdiction, there is generally present the utmost cohesion. They are all working with the same definite purpose; therefore, in spite of the number of different religious communities often employed in a diocese, praiseworthy uniformity generally results.

(c) Catholic schools are united.   They are a unit on the necessity of religious education; on obedience to episcopal authority; on the fundamentals of sound educational principles and methods.   Although a great deal of freedom in details is allowed, the acceptances by our schools of the same principles explains why the underlying unity of Catholic education is maintained in spite of diocesan difference in organization and administration.

14. Q. Is there an official national Catholic school organization?

A. Not in the strict sense of the word.   Each diocesan organization controls its own schools.   There is, however, a Department of Education of the National Catholic Welfare Council, under an episcopal chairman, which stands to our schools much in the same relation as the Federal Bureau of Education does to the schools of the United States.

15. Q. What are the functions of the Department of Education of the N. C. W. C.?

A. Its functions are advisory and directive.

It acts—

1. As a clearing house of information concerning Catholic education and Catholic education agencies—for Catholic educators and students, and for the general public.

2. As an advisory agency to assist Catholic educational systems and institutions in their development.

3. As a connecting agency between Catholic education activities and Government education agencies.

4. As an active organization to safeguard the interests of Catholic education.

16. Q. What is the Catholic Educational Association?

A. It is a voluntary organization of Catholic educators, who meet yearly to discuss educational problems.   The

Catholic Educational Association has no administrative authority over the Catholic schools of the United States. The Catholic Educational Association is divided into College, Seminary and Parish School Departments, and into many other sections. It publishes the Proceedings of the Annual Meeting and pamphlets on educational subjects.

REFERENCES

Dunney, *The Parish School,* Macmillan, N. Y., 1921.

Burns, *Growth and Development of the Catholic School System in the United States,* Benziger, N. Y., 1912.

Burns, *Principles, Origin and Establishment of the Catholic School System in the United States,* Benziger, N. Y., 1912.

Burns, *Catholic Education: A Study of Conditions,* Longmans, Green & Company, N. Y., 1917.

Waldron, "The Organization of a Diocesan School System" (*Proceedings C. E. A.,* Vol. XI.).

Gibbons, "School Supervision—Its Necessity, Aims, and Methods" (*Proceedings C. E. A.,* Vol. II.).

Johnson, "Diocesan School Superintendent," *Catholic Education Review,* Washington, 1921.

CHAPTER IV

ORGANIZATION OF THE CATHOLIC SCHOOL SYSTEM

TYPES OF SCHOOLS

1. Q. What are the different types of Catholic schools in the United States?

A. The Catholic schools of the United States follow the same lines of organization as the State-controlled schools. They may be divided into three main classes: Elementary schools, high schools, and colleges.

2. Q. What is an elementary school?

A. Parish schools are ordinarily elementary schools consisting of eight grades.

3. Q. What subjects are taught in parish schools?

A. The curriculum of the parish school has practically the same content as that of the public elementary school—reading, writing, grammar, spelling, arithmetic, history and geography—to which must be added religion. In addition to these subjects some schools embrace others of an elementary character, such as those touching on literature, art, and science.

In some dioceses, especially the larger ones, kindergartens have been added to many of the parish schools.

4. Q. What are institutional schools?

A. By institutional schools we mean orphan asylums, industrial schools, schools for the blind, deaf and dumb asylums, schools for delinquents, and schools for subnormal children. The institutional type of school is fundamentally elementary in character. The standard elementary curriculum in certain cases is revised to meet the subnormalities of the children who attend such schools. Institutional schools are generally boarding schools.

19

5. Q. What are rural schools?

A. Rural schools are country schools, as distinguished from urban or city schools. The curriculum is the same as that of the city school.

6. Q. What school follows the elementary or parish school?

A. The high school. After a child has successfully completed eight grades in the elementary or parish school, he is admitted to the high school. A high school may be a parish high school, intended chiefly for the children of a certain parish, or a central high school, intended for the children of a district or city. There is a tendency in the direction of making high schools central.

7. Q. What is a high school?

A. A high school is an institution which offers a four years' course, following upon eight years of elementary school training. The high school is often called a secondary school to distinguish it from the primary or elementary school.

8. Q. What is a junior high school?

A. The junior high school is an institution which, in addition to the work of the seventh and eighth grades, offers two years of high school training. There are very few junior high schools in the Catholic school system.

9. Q. What are the purposes of a high school?

A. A high school has various purposes:

It offers a course of cultural and informational value, sufficient in itself to prepare boys and girls for an intelligent participation in the work and life of the community.

It trains them by practical and vocational courses for mechanical trades or for business occupations.

Another purpose is to prepare a student for college or for the higher professional schools.

10. Q. Are Catholic high schools co-educational?

A. No. Catholic high schools are not co-educational except when they are parish high schools. Catholic high schools are more or less sharply defined into high schools for boys and high schools for girls. Girls' high schools are generally known as academies.

11. Q. In what way has this division into boys' and girls' high schools affected the Catholic high school?

A. This traditional division has had its effect on the content of the curriculum of each type of high school up to very recent times. Today, however, the general tendency is to offer the same courses to boys and girls.

Most Catholic high schools, both for boys and girls, in addition to the college preparatory courses, offer instruction in commerce, secretarial work, and, in some cases, in vocational and industrial pursuits.

12. Q. What does it mean for a high school to be accredited or affiliated?

A. For a high school to be accredited means that its "credits" are accepted at their full value by a recognized college, State university, or educational association.

Affiliation means practically the same thing. It indicates a closer bond of union between the high school and the college with which the affiliation takes place. The affiliated school becomes closely connected with the central organization or parent institution.

13. Q. Are many Catholic high schools accredited?

A. The great majority of Catholic high schools are accredited to the various State universities, or are affiliated with the Catholic University of America.

14. Q. What is the effect on the high school of being accredited to an institution of higher learning?

A. Accrediting insures uniformity in curriculum, as well as in methods of teaching and in results.

15. Q. What is a college?

A. A college is an institution with a four years' course, following the four years of high school.

16. Q. What is a junior college?

A. A junior college is an institution which offers but two years' collegiate work.

The junior college has not found much favor in Catholic educational circles. It commends itself to those who see in it a means of giving at least two years of Catholic college training to students who intend to enter professional schools.

17. Q. Who are admitted to college?

A. For entrance to college, a student must possess a diploma or certificate from an accredited high school. On graduation from college, the student receives the degree of Bachelor of Arts or of Science, B.A. or B.S.

18. Q. Are Catholic colleges co-educational?

A. As in the high school, there is little or no co-education in Catholic colleges. Catholic colleges are divided into colleges for men and colleges for women.

19. Q. What subjects are taught in Catholic colleges?

A. The curriculum of the Catholic college centres about the liberal arts. In most colleges, however, students are permitted a wide range of "election;" that is, they are allowed, after certain prescribed courses, to select optional subjects for study.

20. Q. Are Catholic colleges standard colleges?

A. Yes; most of our Catholic colleges are standard colleges.

21. Q. What is a standard college?

A. A standard college is one which follows certain definite rules laid down by educational organizations as necessary for the satisfactory accomplishment of work of collegiate grade.

22. Q. What are these educational organizations?

A. The organizations which promulgate these rules are voluntary associations of colleges, or, in some cases, State universities. The Catholic Educational Association, for example, has a set of standards and a list of standard colleges.

This list includes 67 Catholic colleges which have asked for the recognition of the Catholic Educational Association and have been accepted.

23. Q. What colleges are recognized by the Catholic Educational Association as standard?

A. The following colleges are listed as standard (list of 1921):

FOR MEN:

Boston College, Boston, Mass.

Campion College, Prairie du Chien, Wis.

Canisius College, Buffalo, N. Y.

Catholic University of America, Washington, D. C.

College of St. Francis Xavier, Brooklyn, N. Y.

College of St. Thomas, St. Paul, Minn.

Columbia College, Dubuque, Iowa.

Creighton University, Omaha, Neb.

De Paul University, Chicago, Ill.

Duquesne University, Pittsburgh, Pa.

Fordham University, Fordham, N. Y.

Georgetown University, Washington, D. C.

Gonzaga University, Spokane, Washington.

Holy Cross College, Worcester, Mass.

Jefferson College, Convent, La.

Loyola College, Baltimore, Md.

Loyola University, Chicago, Illinois.

Loyola University, New Orleans, La.

Manhattan College, New York City.

Marquette University, Milwaukee, Wis.

Mt. St. Mary College, Emmitsburg, Md.

Spring Hill College, Spring Hill, Ala.

St. Ambrose College, Davenport, Iowa.

St. Benedict College, Atchison, Kansas.

St. Bonaventure College, Allegany, N. Y.

St. Francis' College, Loretto, Pa.

*St. Francis' College, Brooklyn, N. Y.

St. Ignatius' College, Cleveland, Ohio.

St. Ignatius' College, San Francisco, Cal.

St. John College, Brooklyn, N. Y.

St. John University, Collegeville, Minn.

St. John University, Toledo, Ohio.

St. Joseph College, Philadelphia, Pa.

St. Louis University, St. Louis, Mo.

St. Mary College, St. Marys, Kansas.

St. Mary College, Oakland, Cal.

St. Viator College, Bourbonnais, Ill.

*Admitted June, 1921.

St. Xavier College, Cincinnati, Ohio.

University of Dayton, Dayton, Ohio.

University of Detroit, Detroit, Mich.

University of Notre Dame, Notre Dame, Ind.

University of Santa Clara, Santa Clara, Cal.

Villanova College, Villanova, Pa.

FOR WOMEN:

College of St. Catherine, St. Paul, Minn.

College of St. Elizabeth, Convent, N. J.

College of Mt. St. Vincent, New York City.

College of New Rochelle, New Rochelle, N. Y.

College of Notre Dame of Maryland, Baltimore, Md.

College of St. Teresa, Winona, Minn.

College and Academy of Sacred Heart, Cincinnati, Ohio.

D'Youville College and Holy Angels Academy, Buffalo, N. Y.

*Our Lady of the Lake College, San Antonio, Texas.

Loretto Heights College, Loretto, Colo.

Loretto College, Webster Grove, Mo.

Mt. St. Joseph College, Dubuque, Iowa.

*Incarnate Word College, San Antonio, Texas.

St. Clara College and Academy, Sinsinawa, Wis.

*St. Francis Xavier College, Chicago, Ill.

*St. Joseph College, Emmitsburg, Md.

St. Mary College and Academy, Monroe, Mich.

St. Mary College, Notre Dame, Ind.

St. Mary College, Portland, Oregon.

*St. Mary College, Prairie du Chien, Wis.

St. Mary-of-the-Woods College, St. Mary-of-the-Woods, Ind.

*Seton Hill College, Greensburg, Pa.

Trinity College, Washington, D. C..

Mt. St. Mary College, North Plainfield, N. J.

24. Q. What must a college do to be recognized as standard?

A. For a college to be accepted as standard, it must require not less than fifteen "units" for entrance; one hundred and twenty semester hours for graduation; must have eight distinct departments of study; its faculty must consist of at least eight full-time professors, with definite academic qualifications; its library and scientific equipment must be of a certain kind and of a fixed value. Some standardizing agencies require more than the above and some require less. In the main, however, any college which fulfills the above conditions would be recognized as standard.

*Admitted June, 1921.

25. Q. What is a seminary?

A. A seminary is an institution for the education of candidates for the priesthood.

Seminaries are of two kinds, preparatory and theological. The preparatory seminary is equivalent to the junior college. The theological seminary offers a two years' course in philosophy followed by four years of theology, and is therefore the equivalent of the professional school of a university.

26. Q. What is a university?

A. The term designates an institution which, besides a college, maintains also professional schools and confers advanced degrees, as M.A., Ph.D., D.D. The university grew out of the college of liberal arts in the Middle Ages. It is the product of Catholic science and faith.

27. Q. What subjects are taught in a university?

A. The American university has developed a great number of courses in the liberal arts and professional schools, the most important of which are schools of theology, of medicine, law, engineering, pharmacy, dentistry, commerce and finance. Catholic universities have taken part in this development and present much the same character as State or non-sectarian universities.

28. Q. How many Catholic universities are there?

A. There are 16 Catholic institutions in the United States offering work of university grade.

REFERENCES

Burns, *Catholic Education*, Longmans, Green & Company, N. Y., 1917.

Newman, *Idea of a University*, Longmans, Green & Company, N. Y., 1910.

Newman, "Rise and Progress of Universities," Vol. III., *Historical Sketches*, Longmans, Green & Company, N. Y., 1910.

Ryan, *Directory of Catholic Colleges and Schools*, Bureau of Education, N. C. W. C., Washington, 1921.

Waldron, "The Organization of a Diocesan School System" (*Proceedings C. E. A.*, Vol. XI.).

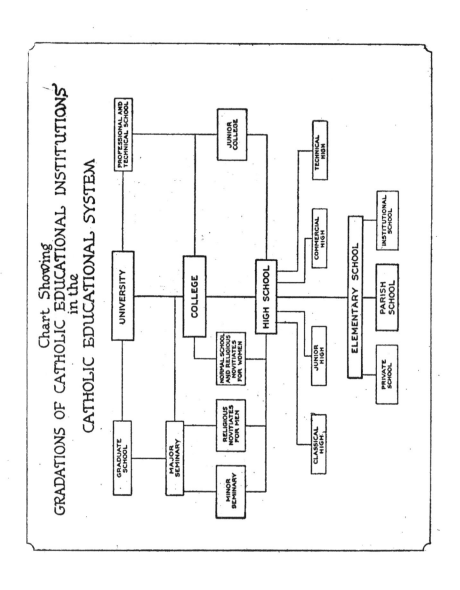

Chart Showing
GRADATIONS OF CATHOLIC EDUCATIONAL INSTITUTIONS
in the
CATHOLIC EDUCATIONAL SYSTEM

CHAPTER V

Teachers in the Catholic School System

1. Q. Who teach in the Catholic schools?

A. Most of the teachers in Catholic schools are members of religious orders or congregations. There is, however, a great number of lay teachers.

2. Q. Are lay teachers welcomed in the Catholic school system?

A. The Department of Education, N. C. W. C., passed the following resolution with reference to lay teachers: "That laymen be encouraged to take a larger share in our educational work, especially by participation as teachers."

3. Q. Why are most of the teachers in Catholic schools members of religious communities?

A. The diffusion of knowledge, especially religious knowledge, has always been regarded as one of the prime functions of the Church of Christ, a continuation of the work of the Apostles themselves, to whom Christ said: "Go, and teach all nations." For that reason she has set aside, and even consecrated, the lives of the men and women whom she selects as teachers.

4. Q. Are there many men teaching in our Catholic schools of religious congregations?

A. Yes, there are about forty religious orders of men whose members teach in the Catholic schools of the United States. Many of the secular clergy also occupy positions as administrators and teachers in our schools.

5. Q. Are all these men priests?

A. No, a great number of men teachers belong to religious brotherhoods.

6. Q. What are religious brotherhoods?

A. Religious brotherhoods are congregations of men bound together by vows. They do not take Holy Orders.

7. Q. What advantages are there in having teachers who are members of religious communities?

A. There are many advantages. In the first place, religious teachers labor from the highest motive, namely, the pure love of God. They receive no personal compensation for their work. They teach because they see in teaching the best service which they can perform for the kingdom of God. The training of children in the knowledge and love of God is their life's object. This holy motive is consecrated by vows taken to God Himself.

Secondly, as a member of a religious community one can consecrate one's whole life to teaching, putting aside any idea of changing or bettering one's position in this world. Neither does a religious teacher worry about his daily needs, as the community provides for them. The consequence is concentration on the purposes of his profession with little or no outside distraction.

Thirdly, as a member of a religious community, the religious teacher is urged and even required constantly to perfect himself in his chosen profession. For the religious, the period of intellectual training never comes to an end. The religious life is a daily development in character-building. The formal study, which he is obliged by rule to indulge in, keeps him constantly abreast of the best educational thought and principles.

Fourthly, the religious teacher, because of his training and his vows, is less individualistic than the teacher in a non-religious system; he therefore more easily fits into a religious system of education and is more ready to accept the guidance of superiors. This is a vital necessity in the Catholic system, which is based upon a definite religious belief and is permeated through and through with a definite ethical teaching.

Fifthly, the religious teacher exerts an unusual influence on his pupils. He embodies in his life and conduct the principles and ideals he professes and inculcates. Personal influence in an inspiring environment is a most effective element of the educational process. The high character of this personal influence is the specific contribution of the religious teacher in the Catholic school.

In a word, the religious teacher is not only a good teacher, but he is a good teacher because he is a religious.

8. Q. Is there a need for more religious teachers?

A. It is one of the crying needs of American Catholic life. Thousands of children today are not receiving the benefits of a Catholic education because the Church cannot supply the religious teachers in numbers sufficient to meet the demand.

9. Q. What can Catholics do to remedy this situation?

A. (a) They can instruct their children in the nobility of the profession of the religious teacher. If any of them evince a desire to enter religion, parents should put no obstacles in their way, but encourage their holy aspirations towards the religious state.

(b) They can contribute generously to the support of seminaries, religious novitiates and normal training schools in which are trained the teachers for our schools.

(c) They can pray God daily to send "more workers into His vineyard."

References

Burns, *Catholic Education,* Longmans, Green & Company, N. Y., 1917.

Schwickerath, *Jesuit Education,* B. Herder Book Company, St. Louis, 1904.

Brother Leo, *St. John Baptist de la Salle,* Kenedy, N. Y., 1921.

Shields, *Philosophy of Education,* Catholic Education Press, Washington, 1910.

CHAPTER VI

Training of Catholic School Teachers

1. Q. What system of professional preparation for teachers is used in the Catholic school system?

A. The Catholic system of training is practically the same as that used for the preparation of public school teachers.

2. Q. Outline the various steps in teacher-training as followed in Catholic training schools.

A. After a period of preparation for the religious state, called a novitiate, a religious teacher takes up the formal work of preparing for the teaching profession. If the novice, as the young religious is called, has completed her high school education, she immediately begins two years of normal training work. If, however, the high school course has not been completed, the novice is obliged to take up the study of high school subjects, until she has satisfactorily finished them. After the completion of her normal training course, the young religious is sent out as a student-teacher.

3. Q. What courses are presented in the Catholic normal training school?

A. The following outline of courses given at the St. Clare School of Education, Winona, Minnesota, is typical of the best Catholic normal training school schedules.

| First Year | | | Second Year | | | Third Year | |
Subject	Semester		Subject	Semester		Subject	Semester
Methods in Religion	I	II	Methods in Religion	I	II	History of Education	I
English ...	I	II	English Literature	I	II	Economics	I
History and Civics ..	I	II	Child Psychology ...		I	Sociology	I
Psychology	I	II	Special Methods	I	II	Supplementary Requirements	I
General Methods	I	II	Mathematics ..	I		Supplementary Lectures ...	I
School Management ..	I		College Algebra		II		
School Organiztion ...		II	Modern Language	I	II		
Natural Science .	I	II				Apprentice Teaching	II

4. Q. Does a religious teacher fulfill all the conditions of professional preparation by graduating from a normal training school?

A. No; she is obliged to attend teachers' institutes, summer courses, and even summer school, although she is acknowledged beforehand to be a competent teacher. A few dioceses offer Teachers' Institutes under diocesan direction. Most of the large communities maintain their own summer schools. The smaller communities attend the extension courses and summer schools conducted by the different Catholic universities and colleges. There were 24 Catholic summer schools in the United States in 1921. The following colleges offered courses open to religious teachers:

Canisius College, Buffalo, N. Y.; Catholic University, Washington, D. C.; Columbia College, Dubuque, Iowa; Creighton University, Omaha, Nebr.; De Paul University, Chicago, Ill.; Fordham University, New York, N. Y.; St. John College, Brooklyn, N. Y.; St. John University, Toledo,

Ohio; Little Rock College, Little Rock, Ark.; St. Louis University, St. Louis, Mo.; Loyola University, Chicago, Ill.; Loyola University, New Orleans, La.; Marquette University, Milwaukee, Wis.; Notre Dame University, Notre Dame, Ind.; College of St. Teresa, Winona, Minn.; Villa Nova College, Philadelphia, Pa.; St. Xavier College, Cincinnati, Ohio.

5. Q. What is the attitude of Catholic educators towards more adequate preparation for the profession of teaching?

A. An attitude of utmost sympathy. During the last decade there has been a notable increase in the number of Catholic teachers attending teacher training schools. After graduating from the normal training school, a great number continue their studies in the college for the purpose of obtaining an academic degree.

If this movement continues for another twenty-five years, there will be few, if any, Catholic teachers who have not had the most thorough professional preparation.

6. Q. What is the relative status of professional preparation of public school teachers and Catholic school teachers?

A. According to Dr. P. P. Claxton, former United States Commissioner of Education, there were 600,000 public school teachers in the United States. "Of these," he states, "about 30,000 have not gone beyond the eighth grammar grade; 100,000 others, not two years further, and 200,000 more, not four years further. Half our teachers have thus had no particular preparation whatever."

Although we have no exact statistics to offer, for the Catholic School System as a whole, it can be fairly estimated that of the 41,581 teachers in Catholic elementary schools, 75 per cent. are graduates of high schools or have had considerable high school training, at least 50 per cent. have had formal teacher training, and practically none is teaching today without a considerable amount of preparation acquired in the class-room and by attendance at summer courses.

Exact figures with reference to the professional training of Catholic school teachers in Wisconsin are available. In an article, "The Certification of Teachers in Wisconsin" (*Proceedings C. E. A.,* 1919), it is pointed out that: "In the State of Wisconsin 42.6 per cent. of teachers reported have training above high school; 37 per cent. have more or less college training; 19.1 per cent. have professional training other than Catholic Community and normal; 74.5 per cent. have high school training, and 25.2 per cent. hold certificates."

Membership in a teaching religious community, since it is permanent, necessarily involves a progressive preparation for teaching. This is impossible for the ordinary lay teacher who must begin her work at an early age and who will not continue it for more than a few years.

7. Q. What is the relative age of teachers in the public school system and in the Catholic school system?

A. The great majority of public school teachers are under twenty-one. Of the 600,000 teachers, about 150,000 serve two years or less, and 300,000 not over four or five years. The average teaching life of a public school teacher is four and a half years. According to Dr. Strayer of Columbia University, 140,000 teachers, or one in five, left the profession in 1919, and one in every ten is young and inexperienced.

Catholic teachers begin teaching as young as public school teachers. They do not, however, leave the profession. The Catholic School System, therefore, has no "age problem." There are no available statistics, but it can be safely asserted that 75 per cent. of the Catholic school teachers are above the age of twenty-five. Of this 75 per cent., at least 50 per cent. are above the age of thirty.

There is no need to point out what this means in stabilizing education and in maintaining a high quality of instruction.

8. Q. What is certification of teachers?

A. It is a process which is employed by the State to testify to the fitness of a candidate for the teaching profession. Different States have different requirements, which must be met before "certificates" or "licenses" to teach are given.

9. Q. How are certificates acquired?

A. Either by examination or by presenting credentials which show the necessary professional training. There is, however, no uniformity in the State laws with reference to the educational prerequisites for certification.

10. Q. Do any States require the certification of teachers in private or parochial schools?

A. A few do. Alabama, Nebraska, and South Dakota require certificates; Kentucky requires that private teachers be approved. In many other States there is a tendency to require certificates of all teachers, public or private.

11. Q. What is the Catholic attitude towards State certification of teachers?

A. There is no uniformity of opinion among Catholic educators. A great number, and the number is constantly increasing, favor reasonable certification requirements. In New York State, in the Middle West, and in the South many religious teachers have applied for State certificates and have received them. In 1919, the Conference of Women's College of the C. E. A. formally approved a plan for the certification of Catholic teachers.

12. Q. What preparation do the members of religious orders of men receive for teaching?

A. (a) The brotherhoods follow the same system of teacher-training as the sisterhoods. The high school teachers prepare for their work by taking college degrees.

(b) Many of the members of religious orders who are priests take, after ordination, university degrees in preparation for the career of professor. They attend either universities conducted by their own order or the Catholic University of America.

References

Burns, *Catholic Education*, Longmans, Green & Company, N. Y., 1917.

Sargent, *American Private Schools*, Boston, 1921.

Schwickerath, *Jesuit Education*, B. Herder Book Co., St. Louis, 1904.

"Certification of Teachers—A Symposium," *Proceedings C. E. A.*, 1919.

State Laws and Regulations Relative to Certification of Teachers, Bureau of Education, N. C. W. C., Washington, 1921.

CHAPTER VII

CURRICULUM OF THE CATHOLIC SCHOOL

1. Q. What is a school curriculum?

A. It is a fixed course of studies.

Each distinct type of school has its own special curriculum. We speak, therefore, of the curriculum of the elementary school, of the high school, of the college.

2. Q. Is there a uniform Catholic parish school curriculum?

A. No; as in the different State systems of education, so in the Catholic system, there are found many divergences in the matter of curriculum. In the main, however, a curriculum of the Catholic school of any given locality closely approximates the curriculum of the public schools of the same locality.

The differences in methods and curricula in the different dioceses are not so wide as to cause educational disorder. All religious communities and, particularly the progressive ones, agree on the basic principles of method and curriculum.

3. Q. What is, then, the main difference in the public school curriculum and in that of the Catholic school?

A. The main difference is in the matter of religious instruction. Every Catholic school teaches religion for a definite period of time each day. Besides this formal instruction, religion is made the basis of all other instruction with which it is correlated and of which it forms the ground-work.

4. Q. Give examples of typical public and Catholic school elementary curricula.

A. The following time schedules of a parish school and a public school show the similarities and differences that exist:

TIME DISTRIBUTION BY SUBJECTS AND GRADES IN FIFTY REPRESENTATIVE CITIES.

Grades				Minutes Per Week				
	I	II	III	IV	V	VI	VII	VIII
Opening Exercises	59	59	59	54	50	48	48	48
Penmanship	78	93	81	82	78	73	60	57
ubc	68	130	73	74	70	70	70	68
Drawing	152	84	87	81	78	78	78	76
...ining	65	73	62	70	78	88	112	115
Science, Physiology, Hygiene, and Nature Study	57	64	62	57	53	62	70	88
Geography	25	11	78	129	158	166	152	118
Arithmetic	93	149	203	221	223	226	217	220
History	42	48	54	88	104	110	141	181
Iugge, Grammar and Composition	116	122	144	164	180	183	208	220
Reading and Phonics	412	364	291	237	195	181	152	150
Spelling	84	102	113	104	95	90	81	79
Physical Training	71	64	62	62	59	62	59	60
Recesses	135	128	128	119	113	109	102	102
Miscellaneous, Unassigned and Study Time	118	97	135	119	122	121	121	135

Table from the Fourteenth Yearbook of the National Society for the Study of Education, University of Chicago Press, 1915.

WASHINGTON, D. C., PUBLIC SCHOOLS—1050-1500 Minutes Per Week In Total Sessions.

Grades	I	II	III	IV	V	VI	VII	VIII
					Minutes Per Week			
Opening Exercises	25	25	50	50	50	50	50	50
Writing	[1]150	75	75	75	75	75	45	45
Music	60	60	60	60	60	60	60	60
Drawing, Art and Construction	60	60	90	90	[2]90	[2]90	[2]90	[2]90
Sewing			45	45	60	90		
Cooking							90	90
Manual Training							90	90
Physiology and Hygiene	15	15	30	30	[3]75	[3]60	[3]60	[3]60
Geography			60	90	120	150	150	[4]105
Nature Study and Elementary Science	60	60	75	80	[3]75	[3]60	[3]60	[3]60
Mathematics: Arithmetic	35	90	215	230	225	185	[5]185	[5]150
Algebra								[6]105
History and Civics	30	40	75	80	90	120	[5]150	[5]150
Language, Grammar and Composition	70	70	100	100	120	150	[5]200	[5]240
Reading and Literature	370	270	250	220	170	120	110	120
Phonics	25	25	25					
Spelling and Word Analysis	60	60	75	75	90	60	60	90
Physical Culture	50	50	75	75	75	75	75	75
Recesses	75	75	125	125	125	125	125	125
Unassigned Time	65	75	75	75	75	75	50	50

1 For Grade 1A the time allotted to writing will be used as unassigned time.
2 Two periods of 45 minutes each, or two periods of 60 minutes and 30 minutes each, at the option of teacher.
3 Equal portions of time divided between Geography and Hygiene and Nature Study and Elementary Science.
4 8A only.
5 With consent of Supervising Principal, a greater time to either Arithmetic, History or Grammar and Composition, provided 30 minutes more than the other subjects named is reduced by this amount.
6 8B only.
7 Not to be permanently assigned to any subject, but to appear on program as unassigned time.
8 Grades I, II, III, IV, two periods daily; Grades V, VI, VII, VIII one period daily.

DIOCESE OF PITTSBURGH TIME SCHEDULE
1919-1920.

1500 Minutes Per Week.

Grades				Minutes Per Week				
	1	2	3	4	5	6	7	8
Religion	250	250	250	250	200	200	150	150
Spoken and Written English	230	230	230	230	250	250	270	270
Vocal Music	100	100	100	100	100	100	100	60
Drawing	100	100	100	90	90	90	90	90
Physiology and Hygiene..	50	50	50	40	40	40	40	40
Geography	..	..	75	100	125	150	150	100
Elementary Science	50	50	50	30	30	30	30	40
Arithmetic	200	200	200	275	250	200	140	200
Algebra	..	..	..	..	..	..	60	60
History	..	..	..	30	90	120	150	150
Civics	..	..	..	20	20	20	20	40
Reading and Literature...	420	420	345	235	205	200	200	200
Recess	100	100	100	100	100	100	100	100

ARCHDIOCESE OF BOSTON APPROXIMATE TIME SCHEDULE.

Aggregate time in minutes per week, to be given in the different subjects of the curriculum.

Grades				Minutes Per Week				
	1	2	3	4	5	6	7	8
Opening and Closing Exercises	60	60	60	60	60	60	60	60
Religion	150	150	150	180	180	180	180	180
Reading and Literature ...	540	480	400	200	180	180	150	140
Spoken and Written English	230	200	200	300	300	250	270	250
Penmanship	80	80	80	100	100	90	90	90
Arithmetic	100	210	210	210	230	220	230	230
History	..	..	..	50	50	120	120	150
Geography	..	..	80	130	130	130	150	150
Music	60	60	60	60	60	60	60	60
Drawing	100	80	80	80	80	80	60	60
Physiology and Hygiene ..	30	30	30	30	30	30	30	30
Physical Exercises and Recess	150	150	150	100	100	100	100	100
Totals	1500	1500	1500	1500	1500	1500	1500	1500
Approximate Home Study per week	..	..	..	150	225	300	500	500

5. Q. Is the curriculum now in use in the elementary schools of the United States satisfactory?

A. Not altogether; many objections are urged against it. The general belief seems to be that it needs "humanizing," so that it will more adequately prepare children for their duties as workers and as citizens.

The curriculum of the Catholic elementary school is showing the influence of these criticisms and is, like the public school curriculum, gradually being changed to meet the new conditions of American life.

6. Give an example of typical public and Catholic high school curricula.

UNITS OF STUDY OFFERED IN CERTAIN HIGH SCHOOLS.

Subjects	North Central Association*	West Philadelphia Catholic H. S. For Boys
Religion		2
English	4	4
Latin	4	4
Greek		1
Mathematics	3	4
History	3	2
Commercial Subjects	1½	7
Physics	1	1
Chemistry	1	1
Modern Languages	2	3
Manual Training	1	
Mechanical Drawing		1½
Botany, Biology or Physiology	½	½
Physical Geography or Natural Science	½	½

NOTE.—Each unit represents 1 recitation period per day for a school year of from 36 to 40 weeks, or approximately 180 periods.

*The figures for the North Central Association represent the result of a summary of reports from 869 schools (U. S. Bureau of Education, Bulletin No. 6, 1915).

PUBLIC HIGH SCHOOLS OF WASHINGTON, D. C.

Subject	Periods Per Week				Minutes Per Week			
Year—	I	II	III	IV	I	II	III	IV
English	5	5	5	5	225	225	225	225
Latin	5	5	5	5	225	225	225	225
Mathematics	5	5	5	5	225	225	225	225
History	5	5	5	5	225	225	225	225
Physical Geography	5				225			
Bookkeeping			5	10			225	450
German	5	5	5	5	225	225	225	225
French	5	5	5	5	225	225	225	225
Spanish		5	5	5		225	225	225
Biology	3	3			135	135		
Typewriting		5	5	5		225	225	225
Chemistry			5	5			225	225
Greek		5	5	5		225	225	225
Physics			5	5			225	225
Mechanical Drawing	3	3	4	3	135	135	180	135
Shorthand			5	5			225	225
Civics and Commercial Law			5	5			225	225
Commercial Geography and Economics			5				225	

NOTE—Pupils carry from 22 to 25 periods per week; each period being 45 minutes in length.

WEST PHILADELPHIA CATHOLIC HIGH SCHOOL FOR BOYS.

Subject	Periods Per Week				Minutes Per Week*			
Year—	I	II	III	IV	I	II	III	IV
Religion	3	3	3	2	135	135	135	90
English	5	5	5	5	225	225	225	225
Latin	5	5	5	5	225	225	225	225
Mathematics	5	5	5	5	225	225	225	225
Ancient History	4				180			
Modern History		3					135	
American History			3					135
Physical Geography	3				135			
Bookkeeping	4		2	3	180		90	135
Spanish		5	5	5		225	225	225
Physiology	3				135			
Typewriting		4	3	3		180	135	135
Chemistry		5				225		
Greek				5				225
Physics				5				225
Mechanical Drawing			4	4			180	180
Shorthand			5	4			225	180
Penmanship			1	1			45	45
Civics & Comm. Law			2	2			90	90
Comm. Geog. & Economics			2	2			90	90

NOTES—Pupils carry 30 periods per week, with Religion, English, and at least two years of Latin, Mathematics and Spanish required.

*On 45 minute period basis; probable that actual period is somewhat less than this.

PHILADELPHIA CATHOLIC HIGH SCHOOLS.

From Report of Parish Schools, 1920-1921.

CATHOLIC GIRLS' HIGH SCHOOL.

General Course—1350 Minutes Per Week.

First Year	*Min.	Per.	Second Year	*Min.	Per.
Religion	180	4	Religion	135	3
English	225	5	English	225	5
Mathematics	180	4	Mathematics	180	4
Science	135	3	Science	90	2
Bookkeeping	135	3	Latin	180	4
Latin	135	3	French or		
History	180	4	Spanish	135	3
Drawing	45	1	Typing	90	2
Music	45	1	Stenography	135	3
Penmanship	90	1	Drawing	45	1
			Music	45	1
			Gymnasium	45	1
			Penmanship	45	1

Third Year	*Min.	Per.	Fourth Year	*Min.	Per.
Religion	90	2	Religion	90	2
English	225	5	English	225	5
Mathematics	180	4	Mathematics	135	3
Chemistry	180	4	Physics	180	4
History	180	4	History and		
Latin	180	4	Civics	135	3
French or			Latin	180	4
Spanish	180	4	French or		
Drawing	45	1	Spanish	180	4
Music	45	1	Drawing	45	1
Gymnasium	45	1	Gymnasium	45	1
			Typing	90	2
			Music	45	1

*Min.—Minutes per week. Per.—Periods per week.

WEST PHILDADELPHIA CATHOLIC HIGH SCHOOL FOR BOYS.

Classical Course 1350 Minutes Per Week.

First Year *Min.	Per.	Second Year *Min.	Per.
Religion 135	3	Religion 135	3
English 225	5	English 225	5
Latin 225	5	Latin 225	5
Ancient Hist....180	4	Spanish 225	5
Mathematics ...225	5	Mathematics ...225	5
Physic. Geog...135	3	Physiology 135	3
Bookkeeping ..180	4	Typewriting ...180	4

Third Year *Min.	Per.	Fourth Year *Min.	Per.
Religion 135	3	Religion 90	2
English 225	5	English 225	5
Latin 225	5	Latin 225	5
Spanish 225	5	Greek 225	5
Mod. History..135	3	Spanish 225	5
Mathematics ...180	4	Amer. Hist....135	3
Chemistry 225	5	Physics 135	3

*Min.—Minutes per week. Per.—Periods per week.

7. Q. Compare the courses offered by two typical colleges—one Catholic and the other non-Catholic.

A. The following tables show the curricula offered by St. Xavier's College, Cincinnati, and Amherst College, Amherst, Massachusetts: ...

COMPARISON OF COLLEGE CREDITS

Courses for A.B. degree at Amherst College, Amherst, Mass., and St. Xavier's College, Cincinnati, Ohio, with semester hour credits. A semester hour is defined as a 50-minute lecture, recitation, class exercise or two-hour laboratory period per week, per semester.

Subjects Required	Amherst College	St. Xavier College
Religion		8
English	6	12
Latin or Greek	12	16
Modern Language	12	16
Science	12	8
Mathematics	8	6
History or Philosophy	6	
History		6
Philosophy		16
Public Speaking	2	
	—	—
Total required subjects	58	88
Total units required for degree	124	128
Units of required subjects	58	88
Units required by majors required	36	0
	—	—
Balance, free electives	30	40

NOTE—Majors are subjects pursued for 6 semester courses (at Amherst College) pursued either consecutively or during junior and senior years. Majors may be chosen from group of required or elective subjects, provided courses fulfill requirements.

Subjects Elective Offered	Amherst College	St. Xavier College
Art	yes	
Astronomy	yes	yes
Biblical Literature	yes	
Biology	yes	yes
Chemistry	yes	yes
Economics	yes	yes
Education		yes
Geology	yes	yes
Greek	yes	yes
History	yes	yes
Latin	yes	yes
Mathematics	yes	yes
Modern Languages	yes	yes
Philosophy	yes	yes
Physics	yes	yes
Political Science	yes	yes
Music	yes	
Sociology		yes

COMPARISON OF COLLEGE CREDITS BY COLLEGE YEARS.

Courses for A. B. degree at Amherst College, Amherst, Mass., and St. Xavier's College, Cincinnati, Ohio, with semester hour credits in required and elective studies for each collegiate year. A semester hour is defined as a 50 minute lecture, recitation, class exercise or two-hour laboratory period per week, per semester.

FRESHMAN YEAR.

Subjects	Amherst	St. Xavier
Religion		2
Latin	6	8
English	6	6
Science		8
Mathematics	8	
Greek or Mathematics		6
Public Speaking	1	2
Electives	12	
Total	33	32

SOPHOMORE YEAR.

Religion		2
Latin	6	8
English		6
Science	6	
History	6	
History or Greek		6
Modern Language	6	8
Public Speaking	1	2
Electives	6	
Total	31	32

JUNIOR YEAR.

Religion		2
Logic		4
Psychology		6
Modern Language		8
Major and Minor Electives		12
*Required Majors	12	
Free Electives	18	
Total	30	32

SENIOR YEAR.

Subjects	Amherst	St. Xavier
Religion		2
Ethics		3
Metaphysics		3
Major and Minor Electives		24
*Required Majors	12	
Free Electives	18	
Total	30	32
Grand Total	124	128

*Required Majors are so called because the course of study at Amherst College must be so arranged that it will include two majors, both of which must be completed in the Senior year. A major subject at Amherst College consists of six semester courses in the same subject pursued during six consecutive semesters, or during the Junior and Senior years.

8. Q. What general conclusions may be deduced from the above comparisons?

A. In the first place, the curricula of the different types of Catholic schools are practically the same as those offered by the more progressive public schools and non-Catholic colleges.

Secondly, while religion holds the first place in the Catholic plan, it is by no means the only subject considered in the curriculum. In the Parish Schools of the Diocese of Pittsburgh 200 minutes are given weekly to the study of religion; in the Archdiocese of Boston the time varies from 150 minutes to 180 minutes. A consideration of time schedules demonstrates the falsity of the charge that a disproportionate amount of time is given to the teaching of religion. We acknowledge, however, that the spirit of religion permeates all the work done in the Catholic classroom. Literature, history, geography are interpreted and understood in the light of religious faith. The child's religious inheritance is accorded first place, and it serves to give life and color to the appreciation of all the schoolroom activities.

The Catholic elementary school curriculum is more conservative than the public school curriculum, insisting on the elements of knowledge and carrying through the training in these subjects up to and including the eighth grade. Catholic schools have been slow to adopt the tendency of present day public education to introduce industrial and vocational subjects into the curriculum after the sixth grade. This policy is not the result of lack of funds so much as a belief that the "old" curriculum is the best, all things considered.

There has been little or no experimentation, so to say, with the Catholic school curriculum. Educational fads and fancies have found but small sympathy with Catholic educational authorities, with the result that there has been practically no disturbance in the Catholic school curriculum during the last quarter of a century.

The curriculum of the Catholic high school or college manifests the same general policy of Catholic education; namely, to insist on fundamentals. The basic studies—language, mathematics, science, history—are emphasized in all Catholic colleges and high schools. Electivism is reduced to a minimum. The retention of Greek, although in most cases an elective, is a clear indication of this adherence to the traditional conception of what the curriculum should be.

REFERENCES

Dunney, *The Parish School,* Macmillan, N. Y., 1921.

Burns, *Catholic Education,* Longmans, Green & Company, N. Y., 1921.

MacEachen, *Teaching of Religion,* Macmillan, N. Y., 1921.

CHAPTER VIII

Reasons for the Existence of Catholic Schools

1. Q. For what reasons has the Catholic Church established a separate system of schools?

A. For the following reasons:

Because the Catholic Church is the divinely appointed custodian of the whole body of revealed religious truth and is charged with the duty of teaching it to all men and to all nations. "Going, therefore, teach all nations." To do this adequately, a separate system of schools in our country is necessary.

Because the child is a moral agent, and his education must therefore be moral in the sense that it must recognize the fact that the child is endowed with an immortal soul and is answerable to God for all his actions.

Because will-training is looked upon by the Church as no less important in the educative process than physical or intellectual training.

Because religious knowledge is itself intrinsically valuable in the process of education.

Because religious training is the best training for a citizen.

Because the Church has, by positive law, made the establishment of schools a matter of religious policy.

2. Q. Does not the public school system accept the necessity of moral training?

A. Theoretically it does, but it does not and cannot give the best moral training, which must be Christian. The public school can train children at most in the natural vir-

tues, and even in this it is not successful. It cannot appeal
to the highest motives, which are spiritual and religious.
Catholic education, which is based on Christian principle,
besides inculcating supernatural virtues, the development
of which every Christian must look upon as fundamental,
gives as well the most efficient training in all the virtues
which make upright, honorable men and women.

3· Q. Explain why moral education is a reason and a
justification for the existence of Catholic schools.

A. In the words of the Bishops' Pastoral: "Education
is a co-operation by human agencies with the Creator for
the attainment of His purpose in regard to the individual
who is to be educated, and in regard to the social order of
which he is a member. Neither self-realization alone nor
social service alone is the end of education, but rather these
two in accordance with God's design, which gives to each
of them its proportionate value. Hence it follows that
education is essentially and inevitably a moral activity, in
the sense that it undertakes to satisfy certain claims
through the fulfillment of certain obligations."

4. Q. Why is the training of the will looked upon as so
important by Catholic educators?

A. Because will makes character, and character is more
important than mind. In fact, a trained mind without a
trained will means a mind without moral training, a mind
that is without defence against evil impulses or evil
solicitations.

The Pastoral Letter says: "An education that quickens
the intelligence and enriches the mind with knowledge, but
fails to develop the will and direct it to the practice of vir-
tue, may produce scholars, but it cannot produce good men.
The exclusion of moral training from the educative process
is more dangerous in proportion to the thoroughness with
which the intellectual powers are developed, because it

gives the impression that morality is of little importance, and thus sends the pupil into life with a false idea which is not easily corrected."

5. Q. Why is Catholic religious knowledge essential for the proper training of the mind?

A. Because religious knowledge is the noblest, the highest, and the most important knowledge which the human mind can acquire.

Because religious knowledge, as taught by Catholic teachers, is a reasonable and reasoned belief, and a thoroughly logical body of doctrine on the highest object of human thought.

Because the study of the Catholic religion introduces the pupil to the great historical Church, the mother of all modern civilized nations.

Because the study of the Catholic religion develops the emotional and esthetic powers of man and directs them aright.

Because an education without religion starves the intellect, the heart, and the esthetic faculties.

6. Q. Why does religious education prepare one for a full and complete citizenship?

A. Citizenship does not consist merely in the intellectual recognition of the rights of a government to rule and of one's duties as a citizen to obey. Good citizenship is founded on the will to obey. It, therefore, demands, besides knowledge, a sense of responsibility, respect for authority, and recognition of the rights of our neighbor, all of which flow naturally from a religious education. By combining into a whole the intellectual, moral, and religious elements in education, the Catholic system is the surest and best medium for the training of loyal, upright, and intelligent citizens.

7. Q. Besides formal religious and moral training, what other things characterize the Catholic school?

A. One of the most prominent characteristics of the Catholic school is its religious atmosphere. The majority of the teachers are members of religious communities, and are known and recognized as such by the children. Their manner and ideals of life are religious. Their garb is religious.

The class-room of the Catholic school is decorated with religious pictures and symbols, thus elevating the tone of the school and helping the children to concentrate on the great purposes underlying Catholic life.

The school is situated next to or in close proximity to the church, emphasizing by this fact the close connection which exists between them. The pastor, by his constant watchfulness over the children and frequent visits to the school, exerts a most powerful influence for good.

In a word, the whole atmosphere of the Catholic school is religious. It is, therefore, an unexcelled medium for instruction in the truths of faith and for the development of character in each child who has the privilege of attending it.

8. Q. Can the Sunday School or the religious vacation school supply all the religious knowledge or moral training necessary for citizenship?

A. Both the Sunday School and the religious vacation school are mere makeshifts in the process of educating children religiously. Every educator, and especially every clergyman, appreciates this today.

Thousands of children do not and cannot be made to attend Sunday School. Those who do, are apt to view religion as a subject out of all relation to everyday life. They will likely look upon it as a Sunday affair, not closely related to their week-day experiences. But if religion is to be vital, it should be correlated, both with life and the

week-day school.   It must be taught, and it must be prac-
ticed, every day in the week, not on Sunday only.

George Wharton Pepper in *A Voice From the Crowd*
(page 100), writes: "It is my earnest desire to express
hearty approval of Sunday Schools and to record my admiration for much of their work. At the same time, however, I wish to register my conviction that they cannot be
a final solution of the problem of Christian education. The
Sunday School is, in the last analysis, an agency which at-
tempts on one day in seven to repair the damage systematically done to the Christian theory of life during the other
six.   There should not be in a Christian community two co-
existing educational systems, one developed upon the theory that life and the universe are complete without God,
and the other upon the theory that both life and the universe are merely the sphere of God's self-revelation."

A writer in the Bulletin of the Presbyterian Board of
Publications and Sunday School Work, 1920, says: "The
Daily Vacation Bible School cannot fill all the gap. It
can only fill the gap in vacation time. It leaves the school
year with the burden of religious education carried by the
Sunday School—a Sunday School meeting one hour a
week. The Religious Education Division of the Inter-
Church World Movement reports that the 1,600,000 Jewish
children in the United States receive an average of 250
hours' religious education annually. The 8,000,000 Catholic children receive 200 hours of religious education annually. But the Protestant children receive an average of
only 26 hours of religious education annually. What we
supremely value we take pains to pass on to our children.
Do the Jews prize their religion so much more highly than
Protestants? Do the Catholics realize the value of their
religious heritage so much more than the Protestants?
Here is an appalling failure of Protestantism, a failure that
threatens its life."

9. Q. Is the lack of adequate moral training a grave defect in the American educational system?

A. Yes; it is estimated that less than one-half of the 53,000,000 children of the United States have any religious instruction whatsoever.

10. Q. Is this view with reference to the necessity of religious education peculiar to Catholics?

A. No; the Pastoral Letter says: "There is reason to believe that this conviction is shared by a considerable number of our fellow-citizens who are not of the Catholic faith. They realize that the omission of religious instruction is a defect in education and also a detriment to religion."

11. Q. Give some statements from non-Catholic sources which would bear out this assertion of the Pastoral Letter.

A. George Washington says, in his Farewell Address: "Of all dispositions and habits which lead to political prosperity, religion and morality are indispensable supports. . . . Whatever may be conceded to the influence of refined education on minds of peculiar structure, reason and experience both forbid us to expect that national morality can prevail in exclusion of religious principle."

Edmund Burke: "True religion is the foundation of society. When that is once shaken by contempt, the whole fabric cannot be stable or lasting."

George Bernard Shaw, the English author (*Christian Science Monitor,* January 14, 1921): "If you will have people legislating without any religious foundation, you will get the sort of thing we had from 1914-1920. The only remedy for war is conscience, and you will not have that until you have religion carefully taught and inculcated."

Daniel Webster: "Knowledge does not comprise all that is contained in the large term 'education.' The feelings are to be disciplined; the passions are to be restrained;

true and worthy motives are to be instilled, and pure morality inculcated under all circumstances. All this is com-
prised in education."

Former Vice-President Marshall in a speech at Quincy,
Ill. (*Western Catholic,* June 11, 1920): "Never in the history of the world has there been a time like the present,
when honest men so honestly confessed that government
does not hang upon constitutions and leagues of nations,
but depends upon the gospel of Christ for its salvation.
The real evil of the Church today is that it has turned over
too many of its functions to the State."

Hon. Arthur Balfour to the National Society in London
(St. Paul *Bulletin,* October 23, 1920): "The division between religious and secular training is fundamentally er-
roneous. It implies a dualism of object, a divided object,
which no thinking man, whatever his views are, can really
approve. If religious training is a good thing, do not at-
tempt to divorce it from the general training of the mind.
Do not put it into a separate compartment, as it were, to
be dealt with on entirely different principles and for entirely different purposes. The training of the young people of the country is and must be an organic whole. You
cannot cut it into separate compartments. A school is not
and ought not to be a place merely for filling to the brim
some unfortunate child with what is called a secular
learning."

Marion L. Burton, President of Michigan University, to
the students of the University of Minnesota: "If religion
is to be sovereign, it means that you must cultivate it. The
religious problem is different from the scientific problem;
it is only by practice of the spiritual point of view that the
appreciation of the highest living is achieved. Though we
need criticism and friendship in our life as students, there
is nothing that we need more than religion—the friendship
of God."

'Robert Ellis .Thompson in *The Divine Order of Human Society,* Philadelphia, 1891 (page 171): "I think it open to question whether church schools would not be a better system. In taking this ground, I am not influenced by any view of the State which would unfit it for educating the children of the country in any subject which it is fitting that they should learn. The State is competent to teach what the Church ought to teach. But the Church, through its clergy, can bring to bear an authority in education of a highly ethical kind, which it is not easy for laymen to exert. It can supplement or replace the parental authority more readily than a force of lay teachers. And it is less likely than they to be swayed by the intellectual fashions of the time and the place, less likely to accept as its divinity the spirit of the age, because committed to a preference for what Jean Paul calls 'the spirit of all the ages.'"

Dr. S. Parkes Cadman at Central Y. M. C. A., Brooklyn, December 10, 1920: "Religious education is the largest task that faces the world. Culture alone cannot save mankind. If it could, Athens today would be the centre of civilization. There can be no foundation of democracy except upon the fear and love of God, which is the beginning and end of all wisdom."

Dr. Nicholas Murray Butler, in an address given at the Good Shepherd Church (Episcopal), Augusta, Ga., and reported in the Augusta *Chronicle:* "A new element has taken its place in the world. We are face to face with a teaching that holds Christianity to be not only an illusion and a superstition, but a fraud invented to gain control over men. This you will read in every tract of the Socialists, in every publication of the Bolshevists.

The virtues of charity, humility, service, are held by them to be worthy only of the attention of children, and the world must get along without them; from life must be excluded everything that partakes of religious belief and organization.

One would say that such a plan could not succeed at this late date. Anything is possible today. The human mind was never more credulous than it is now. Never were people so easily moved.

While we are comforting ourselves that, although there may be a storm, the structure that has been built on such a foundation, and founded so securely, cannot be shaken, we forget that the protection is not by faith alone, but by men who are to be leaders as well.

We overlook the fact that instead of being an incidental, education is an essential part of civilization and Christianity. So fundamental it is that it goes back to the time when the father instructed the boy in how to hunt and fish, and make clothes, and when the mother taught her daughter how to take care of the place called home, and how to cook."

National Council of Education, February 28, 1921, at Atlantic City, adopted this resolution: "In view of the dependence of democracy on religion and the attacks to which all churches and all democratic governments are alike being subjected by radicals and radical nations, it is the duty of all churches, irrespective of divergences of creed, to unite in an effort to make religious education more universal and efficient; to emphasize the democratic element in religious instruction; to correlate religious instruction and all elements in public school education helpful to religion; it is the duty of public school authorities to emphasize all non-religious elements in instruction, which tend to make religious instruction more intelligent and efficient, and to organize some systematic form of moral instruction in every public school, and it is the duty of churches and public schools alike to make earnest effort to insure a more general reverence for Divinity and respect for all things religious, including respect for churches other than one's own, and for everything connected with their form of worship."

George Wharton Pepper in *A Voice From the Crowd,* Yale University Press, 1915 (page 124): "The Roman Catholic Church is the religious group which has perceived most clearly the dangers of a secularized education. Not content with protest and lamentation, these brethren of ours have undertaken protective measures for themselves and their children. As is well known, they have established a graded school system of their own throughout the country. I have heard it estimated that in these schools they are giving instruction to about 1,300,000 children. In the meantime, they are paying to the several States their full share of the taxes for the maintenance of public schools. In other words, the Roman Catholic community is simultaneously supporting two systems of public education. I know next to nothing about their financial resources, but it is safe to assume that before long the time will come when such a burden can no longer be carried. When that time arrives, the question will be whether their insistence upon popular religious education will be given up or whether a determined political effort will be made to reform our public school system. It requires little prophetic vision to foresee that it is the latter alternative that will be adopted."

Editor of the St. Louis *Globe-Democrat,* March, 1920: "The Pastoral Letter of the Archbishops and Bishops of the Catholic Church might have been signed by every man professing faith in the Christian religion in all its variants. It is the foundation, the only foundation, of a social order fit to endure. Education without religion; science without religion; culture without religion, serve but to lead mankind into competition, confusion, and strife. The recent Great War was what ought to be the final and complete warning to the world of what must result from national ambition and policies not founded upon and directed by the principles of religion, and especially the religion which has given the Golden Rule as the chief guide for the acts of men."

Mr. Asquith: "I admit as a practical man that denominational schools are an indispensable part of our educational system. You cannot get rid of them because you cannot find any practical substitute for them."

Editor of the New York *Times*, March, 1910: "The movement of the Roman Catholics to secure a system of education which shall not ignore religion is a movement in the right direction. Their self-sacrificing effort in maintaining their parochial schools for this purpose ought to cause us Protestants to blush, when it is compared with our own indifference in this matter. The religious training of Protestant children is left almost entirely to the Sunday School, where the great bulk of the teachers are so inefficient and indifferent that they exert no moral influence over their charges. The bitterness which has existed between Protestants and the Romanists has become so much a matter of the past that it ought to be possible to agree upon some plan whereby our youth can receive some kind of religious training in the public schools. Surely every Christian will rejoice to have such religion given, so that our children will not grow up wholly irreligious and thus become a menace to the well-being of society."

Roger Babson, the great statistician, recently sent the following letter to 16,000 executives as a part of the regular service of his organization: "The need of the hour is not more factories or more materials, not more railroads or steamships, not more armies or more navies, but rather more education based on the plain teachings of Jesus. The prosperity of our country depends on the motives and purposes of the people. These motives and purposes are directed in the right course only through religion. Legislation, bounties, or force are of no avail in determining man's attitude toward life. Harmony at home and peace with the world will only be determined in the same way.

Religion, like everything else of value, must be taught. It is possible to get more religion in industry and business only through the development of Christian education and leadership. With the forces of evil backed by men and money, systematically organized to destroy, we must back with men and money all campaigns for Christian education.

We are willing to give our property and even our lives when our country calls in time of war. Yet the call of Christian education is today of even greater importance than was ever the call of the army or the navy. I say this because we may at any time see our best institutions attacked from within.

I am not offering Christian education as a protector of property because nearly all the great progressive and liberal movements of history have been born in the hearts of Christian educators. I do, however, insist that the safety of our sons and daughters, as they go out on the streets this very night, is due to the influence of preachers rather than to the influence of policemen and law makers. Yes, the safety of our nation, including all groups, depends on Christian education. Furthermore, at no time in our history has it been more greatly needed.

We insure our houses and factories, our automobiles and our businesses through mutual and stock companies, but the same amount of money invested in Christian education would give far greater results. Besides, Christian education can insure what no corporation can insure—namely, prosperity.

As the great life insurance companies are spending huge sums on doctors, scientific investigations and district nurses to improve the health of the nation, so we business men should spend huge sums to develop those fundamental religious qualities of integrity, faith and service, which make for true prosperity. I repeat, the need of the hour is—not more factories or materials, not more railroads or steamships, not more armies or navies—but rather more Christian education. This is not the time to reduce investments in schools and colleges at home, or in similar work in China, Japan, Russia or South America. This is the time of all times to increase such subscriptions."

12. Q. Is then religion necessary to national progress?

A. Yes; without religion a nation cannot go forward. Wealth may accumulate, but mankind will decay. This is the incontrovertible verdict of all history. Religion must be the very backbone of a nation, and religion can be learned only in the schools. As the school, so the nation.

13. Q. What is, beyond question, the most important part of education?

A. To train children to put in practice the moral and religious principles which they learn at school. •

14. Q. Do not Catholic schools exaggerate the importance of religion by giving a disproportionate amount of time to its study?

A. They do not. A relatively small amount of time is given weekly to the formal study of religion, never more than one-sixth of the fifteen hundred minutes allowed to all subjects. Religion is, however, always accorded first place and is never divorced either from the curriculum or from life. Besides the formal study of religion, religious practices and habits are taught and inculcated. "To seek first the kingdom of God" is the basis of all Catholic pedagogy as well as of all Catholic life.

Present day conditions are such that the school must insist more rather than less on religion. The decline in

morality, both individual and social, which is characteristic of post-war times, imposes upon the Catholic school
the burden of teaching this generation a standard of ethics
not generally accepted by the irreligious or non-religious
masses amongst which they must live. In doing this, our
schools are not only preserving the faith of our children
and raising up devout followers of Christ, which is the
highest aim of education, but they are at the same time
educating upright citizens for the Republic.

The need of adequate moral training for all our American children is more than self-evident. Not only Catholic,
but non-Catholic children as well, must receive a definite
moral education if our democratic institutions are to endure. The nation need fear little from outside aggression.
It cannot, however, stand if its own citizens manifest dis-
respect for law and order because of ignorance of what is
moral and immoral. This is true of every kind of government. It is doubly true in a democracy where the people
rule. In a democracy, high moral standards are manifestly
impossible if the people are ignorant of what true morality
is and have not been trained from childhood in its principles and practices.

**15. Q. Cite the laws of the Church with reference to the
necessity of religious education and the establishment of
Catholic schools.**

A. From the syllabus of Pius IX, December 8, 1864, this
proposition may be cited amongst those which are con-
demned: "48· Catholics may approve of a system of education which is separated from the Catholic faith and the
power of the Church and which concerns itself with the
knowledge of merely natural things and only, or at least
primarily, with the ends of social life."

From the Instruction addressed to the American Bishops,
November 24, 1875: "There is nothing so necessary as
that Catholics should have schools of their own, and these

in no wise inferior to the public schools. No pains, therefore, are to be spared to found Catholic schools where they are wanting, to enlarge and equip and arrange them more and more perfectly that they may be put on an equality with the public schools, both in their teaching and managements."

From the First Plenary Council of Baltimore, May 9, 1853: "We exhort the bishops that they take steps to establish a parish school in connection with every church of their diocese."

From the Third Plenary Council of Baltimore, November 9, 1884: "We not only exhort Catholic parents with paternal affection, but we command them with all the authority in our power to procure a truly Catholic education for their dear children and to send them to the parish or other truly Catholic schools.

All Catholic parents are bound to send their children to the parish school unless it is evident that a sufficient training in religion is given either in their own home or in other Catholic schools."

The new Code of Canon Law ordains (Canon 1113): "Parents are bound by a most grave obligation to provide to the best of their ability for the religious and moral, as well as for the physical and civil, education of their children and for their temporal well-being."

(Canon 1372) "From childhood, all the faithful must be so educated that not only are they taught nothing contrary to faith and morals, but that religious and moral training takes the chief place."

(Canon 1375) "The Church has the right to establish schools of every grade, not only elementary schools, but high schools and colleges."

(Canon 1379) "It is desirable that a Catholic university be founded wherever the public universities are not imbued with Catholic teaching and feeling."

Letter of Benedict XV, addressed to the American Episcopate, August 10, 1919: "Nor is the Catholic education of children and youth a matter of less serious import, since it is the solid and secure foundation on which rests the fulness of civil order, faith and morality. You are indeed well aware, Venerable Brethren, that the Church of God never failed on the one hand to encourage most earnestly Catholic education, and on the other vigorously to defend and protect it against all attacks; were other proof of this wanting, the very activities of the Old World enemies of Christianity would furnish conclusive evidence. Lest the Church should keep intact the faith in the hearts of little children, lest her own schools should compete successfully with public anti-religious schools, her adversaries declare that to them alone belongs the right of teaching, and trample under foot and violate the native rights of parents regarding education; while vaunting unlimited liberty, falsely so-called, they diminish, withhold, and in every way hamper the liberty of religious and Catholic parents as regards the education of their children. We are well aware that your freedom from these disadvantages has enabled you to establish and support with admirable generosity and zeal your Catholic schools, nor do We pay lesser meed of praise to the superiors and members of the Religious Communities of men and women who under your direction have spared neither expense nor labor in developing throughout the United States the prosperity and efficiency of their schools. But, as you will realize, We must not so far trust to present prosperity as to neglect provision for the time to come since the weal of Church and State depends entirely on the good condition and discipline of the schools, and the Christians of the future will be those and those only whom you will have taught and trained."

16. Q. What conclusions may we draw from these laws?

A. (a) The Church, in order to be true to her divine mission, must establish schools. Her commission "to teach all nations" authorizes the Church to teach the truths of salvation to every person, whether adult or child, rich or poor, private citizen or public official.

(b) If the Church has the duty of establishing schools, Catholics have the correlative duty of sending their children to these schools.

(c) Catholics, where Catholic schools exist, should not send their children to schools where the teaching of religion is abandoned or the teaching of morality excluded from the curriculum.

(d) If religious education is to continue, the Catholics of America must not swerve in their allegiance to the principles laid down by the Church.

(e) The future both of the Church and of our Country depends upon our allegiance to the religious ideal in education.

REFERENCES

Pastoral Letter of the American Hierarchy, National Catholic Welfare Council, Washington, D. C., 1919.

Burns, *Principles, Origin, and Establishment of the Catholic School System in the United States,* Benziger, N. Y., 1912.

Blakely, *Some Documents on the School Question,* America Press, N. Y., 1921.

CHAPTER IX

Attitude of Catholics Toward the Public School

1. Q. Are Catholics "opposed" to public education?

A. Catholics are not "opposed" to public education. They recognize the need of public education. They also acknowledge that the State has rights in the education of its citizens. They pay their proportionate share of taxes for the upkeep of the public school system. They cannot, however, regard as ideal a system of education which minimizes moral training and excludes religion. They cannot accept the present system of public education as suitable for their children because it does not give to Catholic children the moral and religious training which they must have. They feel free, as every citizen does, to criticize and if need be to condemn, any institution which is the creation of the State and is supported by taxation upon all classes of people. To say, therefore, that Catholics are "opposed" to public education is either to misunderstand the position of the Church on education or to view her attitude with a prejudiced mind.

2. Q. If Catholics are not "opposed" to the public schools, why do they not send their children to them?

A. (a) As a matter of fact, a great number of Catholic children, because of the lack of Catholic schools, do attend the public school. Catholic parents, however, believe that the religious education of their children must be safeguarded at any sacrifice. From the Catholic point of view, attendance at Catholic schools, wherever possible, is the only ideal situation because in some countries the State schools are anti-religious and in other countries they are non-religious, as they are in the United States.

Since education and religion are so inextricably interwoven in any complete system of education, for the State to insist on Catholic attendance at a public school would be an invasion of the fundamental rights of conscience of those who believe that their children must be educated in religion as well as in other subjects. By law the State must refuse to provide for the religious education of our children. Therefore, because of this provision of the Constitution of the United States, "Every Catholic child in a Catholic School" can be our only safe policy.

(b) The fact that thousands of Catholic men and women teach in the public schools would be evidence enough of the fact that we do not "oppose" public education.

(c) Non-attendance at the public school is an immemorial right which we exercise as American citizens— namely, the right to educate our children as our conscience dictates. A number of religious bodies—for example, the Lutherans, Episcopalians and Jews — maintain parish schools. There are a great number of private schools founded and conducted by individuals. Thousands of of American non-Catholic children attend private or denominational schools in every State in the Union. Practically every Protestant religious organization provides for the higher education of its membership outside of State institutions. Of the 119 colleges east of the Mississippi 109 are under religious management; 300 of the 400 standard colleges in the United States are Christian colleges; more than three-fourths of the college students in the United States are in religious colleges.

As long as these schools and colleges obey the laws of the State with reference to education and maintain the standards of efficiency required of the modern school, the organizations which conduct the same are only exercising a right which morally, as well as legally and historically, belongs to them as American citizens. To say, therefore, that an organization is "opposed" to the public school because it maintains its own schools is to indict every religious body in the United States as un-American.

3. Q. Do Catholics then recognize the right of the State to educate?

A. Yes. The Pastoral Letter says: "In accordance with this purpose (of the Constitution) the State has a right to insist that its citizens shall be educated. It should encourage among the people such a love of learning that they will take the initiative and, without constraint, provide for the education of their· children. Should they, through negligence or lack of means, fail to do so, the State has the right to establish schools and take other legitimate means to safeguard its vital interests against the dangers which result from ignorance."

4. Q. Who, according to Catholic teaching has the primary duty towards the education of the child?

A. The parent has the primary duty in the education of the child. This right is fundamental and cannot be delegated to any one else. "Parenthood," says the *Pastoral*, "because it means co-operation with God's design for the perpetuation of human kind, involves a responsibility and therefore implies a corresponding right to prepare for complete living those whom the parent brings into the world."

5. Q. Does the school relieve the parent of this responsibility?

A. The school does not relieve the parent of any responsibility. "The school cannot deprive the parent of his right nor absolve him from his duty in the matter of the education of his children."—*(Pastoral Letter.)*

6. Q. Does the State accept this philosophy of education which we hold?

A. Practically it does. It has wisely never hampered private initiative in education. The results have been worthy of the liberty accorded to each citizen, to follow the dictates of his conscience in the matter of religion and of education.

Religious education has always been and is today very strong in the United States. It has produced the highest type of citizenship. It has at all times intensified loyalty. It has always accepted the educational requirements which the State has demanded of its own schools. The State, moreover, has nothing to fear from the religious school. American statesmen and legislators recognize this fact. As in the past, so now, they look askance at the efforts constantly being made by bigots to do away with the religious school or to injure its work in one way or another.

7. Q. Is this liberty of education a good thing for America?

A. Liberty of education is one of the foundation stones of our democratic government. We have always opposed State monopoly of every kind. State monopoly in education would be the greatest calamity that could happen to the American people.

8. What would be some of the results of State monopoly in education?

A. State monopoly in education would entail the following results:

(a) The end of all educational freedom.

(b) The establishment of a bureaucratic control of our schools.

(c) The death of private initiative in education.

(d) The introduction of politics into the school system.

(e) Increased expenditures of public moneys with little or no increased efficiency in education as a result.

(f) Multiplication of jobs and office holders in the school system—a direct menace to political freedom.

(g) Arbitrary educational rules, policies and laws issued by a central bureau.

(h) Interference with the rights of parents and of children in matters of conscience.

(i) The school would be used as a means of propagating political theories acceptable to those in power. Partisanship in politics would control education.

In a word, the school would be "Sovietized."

9. Q. Give the official statements of the Church with reference to attendance of Catholic children at public schools.

A. From instructions issued by Pope Pius IX, July 14, 1864: "Let all be convinced it is for their greatest interest, not only as individuals and members of families, but also as citizens of that most flourishing American nation, which affords such grounds of hope to the Church, that religion and piety should not be expelled from their schools.

"On the other hand, the Sacred Congregation is not ignorant that sometimes circumstances are such that Catholic parents may conscientiously commit their children to the public schools. But this they cannot do unless for so acting they have a sufficient reason, and whether in any particular case such sufficient reason does not exist must be left to the conscience and judgment of the Bishops. And, according to what is herein detailed, this reason will generally be judged to exist when either there is no Catholic school in the place or the school at hand is but little fitted to give the children an education suited to their condition and circumstance.

"But all parents who neglect to give their children this necessary training and education, or who permit their children to frequent schools in which the ruin of souls cannot be avoided, or, finally, who, having in their locality a good

Catholic school, properly appointed to teach their children, or having the opportunity of educating their offspring in another place nevertheless send them to public schools, without sufficient reason and without the necessary precautions by which the approximate danger may be made remote—these, as is evident from Catholic moral teaching, if they are contumacious, cannot be absolved in the Sacrament of Penance."

From the Third Plenary Council of Baltimore, 1884: "Therefore, we not only exhort Catholic parents with paternal affection, but we *command* them with all the authority in our power to procure a truly Catholic education for their dear children, given them by God, reborn to Christ in Baptism and destined for Heaven; and, further, to defend and secure them from the dangers of secular education throughout the whole time of infancy and childhood; and, finally, to send them to the parish for other truly Catholic school, unless, indeed, the Bishop of the diocese judge that in a particular case other provision may be permitted ... that *all Catholic parents are bound to send their children to the parish school,* unless it is evident that a sufficient training in religion is given either in their own homes or in other Catholic schools or when, because of a sufficient reason, approved by the Bishop, parents have been allowed to send their children, with all due precautions and safeguards, to other schools. What constitutes a Catholic school is left to the decision of the Bishop."

. From the New Code of Canon Law; Canon 1113. "Parents are bound by a most grave obligation to provide to the best of their ability for the religious and moral as well as for the physical and civil education of their children, and for their temporal well-being."

Canon 1372. "From childhood all the Faithful must be so educated that not only are they taught nothing contrary to faith or morals, but that religious and moral training takes the chief place."

Canon 1373. "In every elementary school religious instruction, adapted to the age of the children, must be given."

Canon 1374. *"Catholic children must not attend non-Catholic, neutral, or mixed schools, that is, such as are also open to non-Catholics. It is for the Bishop of the place alone to decide, according to the instructions of the Apostolic See, in what circumstances and with what precautions attendance at such schools may be tolerated, without danger of perversion to the pupils."*

10. Q. In what spirit are Catholic schools maintained in the United States?

A. "Our Catholic schools are not established and maintained with any idea of holding our children apart from the general body and spirit of American citizenship. They are simply the concrete form in which we exercise our rights as free citizens in conformity with the dictates of conscience. Their very existence is a great moral fact in American life. For, while they aim, openly and avowedly, to preserve our Catholic faith, they offer to all our people an example of the use of freedom for the advancement of morality and religion."—*(Pastoral Letter.)*

REFERENCES

Cardinal O'Connell, "The Reasonable Limits of State Activity," *Proceedings C. E. A., 1919.*

Pastoral Letter of the American Hierarchy, N. C. W. C., Washington, D. C., 1919.

Blakely, *Some Documents on the School Question,* America Press, N. Y., 1921.

CHAPTER X

AMERICANISM OF THE CATHOLIC SCHOOL

1. Q. Are Catholic schools American schools?

A. They are American in the true meaning of the term.

To contrast the private school with the public school by calling one American and the other un-American is to reveal both ignorance of the history of education in the United States and of the purposes and ideals which have always actuated the private, and especially the Catholic, schools of the United States.

Neither is the private school un-American because it is an "immigrant school," as the author of *A Stake in the Land* writes. As a matter of fact, more foreign-born children, as well as the children of foreign-born parents, attend the public than the Catholic schools. If, however, it is un-American to educate foreign children in the American way and according to the best American standards, then the Catholic school would be un-American.

2. Q. Why is the Catholic school American?

A. The Catholic school is American for the following reasons:

(a) Its history is American. Catholic schools antedate the American Revolution. They have grown pace by pace with the growth of the country. Catholic schools are not a foreign importation.

(b) Its curriculum is American. The Catholic school

follows the accepted American curriculum from the elementary school to the university.

(c) Its teachers are Americans. The nation has no better or truer citizens than the religious men and women who teach in the Catholic schools.

(d) Its students are Americans or in the process of Americanization.

(e) Its language is the English language.

(f) It is not socialistic, anarchistic or bolshevistic.

(g) Its ideals are American. The Catholic school believes in America, teaches love and respect for America, and has proven its loyalty in every crisis in the nation's history.

(h) Its teaching of religion and of practical morality is American, true to the traditions of the Founders of the Republic.

3. Q. How does the history of the Catholic school prove that it is American?

A. The first American schools were religious schools. The same can be said of our great American colleges. For over two hundred years after the settlement of the English colonies all the schools were church schools, and many of these were Catholic. The same is true of the Spanish and French settlements, where all the schools were Catholic. The tax-supported public school, as a system of State education, dates from 1850, and has, therefore, no claim to being considered the only true American system of education. Since the very beginnings of the Republic the private school, and especially the church-endowed school, has carried the burden of educating great numbers of American children. It is today continuing that work in the same spirit in which it was begun by the early colonists and settlers as well as by the Fathers of the American Republic.

4. Q. How is the curriculum of the Catholic school proved American?

A. The curriculum of the Catholic school in the secular branches is practically the same as that of the public school. A glance at Chapter VII will bear out this statement.

5. Q. How do the teachers in the Catholic school system prove its Americanism?

A. Practically every male teacher in our Catholic schools is an American citizen. The great majority of women teachers, most of them members of religious communities, are either native-born Americans or, since the passage of the Suffrage amendment, have taken out their citizenship papers. The general policy of Catholic education has always been to insist on American citizenship as a prerequisite to teaching in our schools.

6. Q. How do the students in the Catholic school prove the Americanism of the same?

A. In many ways. They prove it by their ideals and their life. They are always loyal and true American citizens who love and respect their country. No socialists or bolshevists are bred in Catholic schools. With reference to this point, the Editor of the *Brooklyn Daily Eagle* well said: "Long controversies have been waged in the past over church schools, but there is at least this to be said for them, that none of the young socialists and incipient revolutionists who are now seen as a danger received their training in such schools. The root of this revolutionary teaching is agnosticism or a thinly veiled atheism. Faith in God and reverence for God make for the respect and observance of moral and social law, and the need for religious training is seen clearly at a time when men and women go about seeking to overturn the foundation of the moral and social order."

The religious school has produced some of the greatest Americans. Washington, Webster, McKinley and Roosevelt were the products of religious schools. Of the Presidents of the United States, sixteen were educated in religious colleges. Of the Justices of the Supreme Court, seven of the eight college men were educated in religious colleges. Amongst the great Americans of our own days, students of the Catholic school from the elementary to the university, none were more American than the late Edward Douglas White and Cardinal Gibbons.

In the Great War the Catholic school engaged in every form of national aid and endeavor. It also sent its product, the parish school boy, into the service in numbers out of all proportion to the strict demands of loyalty.

7. Q. How does the language of the Catholic school prove it to be American?

A. The language of the Catholic school is English. In some Catholic schools the teaching of a foreign language is allowed. This arrangement has distinct educational value. It brings to the child the culture of the race of his forebears and the advantages of a working knowledge of more than one tongue. In all Catholic schools the basic language is English. The Catholic educational policy is to insist that all subjects be taught in English, not excepting religion. It is necessary, however, to permit the teaching of religion both in English and in a foreign language in classes of the children of lately arrived immigrants who cannot understand English or whose parents insist that the Catechism at least be taught them in their mother tongue.

8. Q. In the great majority of Catholic schools is not the instruction given wholly in a foreign language?

A. No. The Catholic schools in which the instruction is given wholly in a foreign language are very few and are becoming fewer every year. The policy of the Church in this matter has not been to force the issue, but slowly to await the opportune time when each foreign group is prepared for the acceptance of the English language. In this way it has not offended the racial sensibilities of the immigrant and has succeeded in transforming the foreign language school, within a relatively short period, into a school where the English language is the sole medium of instruction. Results have proved the wisdom of this slow and patient method of attacking a very difficult problem.

9. Q. How does the teaching of religion prove the Americanism of our schools?

A. Religion has always been recognized, since the days of George Washington, as the foundation upon which good government and good citizenship rest. Religion not only teaches belief in God; it likewise inculcates respect for law and order. "Render to Caesar the things that are Caesar's and to God the things that are God's" has always been the motto of the religious school. Socialism, communism or bolshevism has never found a place in Catholic education. "The best offset to bolshevism in America," says the *Christian Herald*, "is sound religious education such as will promote the growth of spiritual motives in the hearts of all who are accessible to good training."

10. Q. What have the Catholics done to bring about a better understanding and appreciation of our American democracy?

A. During the reconstruction period immediately following the war the National Catholic War Council undertook as one of its most important activities a national civic education campaign. This campaign has been carried on and intensified under the National Catholic Welfare Council.

An excellent series of Americanization pamphlets has been utilized in this better citizenship work. The Council has published and distributed more than 1,000,000 copies of the *Fundamentals of Citizenship,* a short text-book explaining the a b c's of American democracy. A catechetical adaptation of the *Fundamentals of Citizenship* has been prepared in the *Civics Catechism on the Rights and Duties of American Citizens.* This Catechism has been published in several foreign languages, the English text appearing in parallel column form with the foreign translation, thereby permitting the stranger in America to read in his own language of the privileges, opportunities and rights of American citizenship, the process of naturalization and the means of acquiring citizenship, and to obtain knowledge of the English language at the same time.

Realizing that in the elementary school system of the United States the subject of Civics has been almost universally neglected and that only 10 per cent of the elementary school graduates eventually reach high school where Civics is formally taught, the N. C. W. C. has made as one of the principal objects of its Americanization work the introduction of the *Civics Catechism* into the 6,551 Catholic elementary schools of the country. In the higher grades of practically all of these schools a simple course in patriotism and civics, emphasizing the elementary facts of government, is now being given.

Community Americanization programs have been organized by the N. C. W. C. in many cities. More than a hundred Catholic papers and periodicals recently co-operated in publishing serially the chapters of the *Civics Catechism.* Many secular papers and foreign language publications have co-operated in this work.

Other Catholic organizations have either co-operated in or initiated citizenship campaigns similar to the one conducted by the N. C. W. C.

11. Q. How has the Americanization work of the N. C. W. C. been received in circles outside the Church?

A. From many sources has come approval of the Council's organized effort to promote better citizenship, both in the schools and elsewhere. Typical of the praise which the Council's efforts have evoked is the following editorial comment from the *Post Intelligencer,* Seattle, Washington (Feb. 14, 1921):

"It is reassuring to other religionists and provocative of public confidence to be assured that the Americanization work of the Welfare Council is free from denominationalism of any kind; that the Council is planning in the most constructive way that it can devise to make Americans, actual and potential, realize that good citizenship is a matter of great concern to them not only on election day, but on every other day. . . . But beyond the immediate work of the Welfare Council is the assurance that the effective machinery of the Roman Catholic Church is exerting its great influence in these fretful days of reconstruction in the direction of better Americanism and better citizenship. The Church itself is international, but its hierarchy and its membership in America are American. This speaks in many ways, but in none more plainly and forcibly than in the work of the Catholic Welfare Council."

Father de Ville, of Gary, Indiana, has stated the Catholic position very well (N. C. W. C. Press Service): "Many methods thus far used have not succeeded in winning our immigrants but in alienating them. With the young men and women there is a natural tendency to learn English because the young immigrant realizes he cannot rise in the business world otherwise. But to strive to force the older immigrants to learn and use English, to cut them off from their own language, is to create a pitiful type of mediocrity that is fatal to that national progress which depends upon the blending of the genius, the musical and literary traditions and propensities of these people with our own."

President-Emeritus Eliot of Harvard has pointed out "as one danger of 'Americanization' the possibility that efforts will be made to reduce the population to something standardized which will be known as the 'American type.' There is no necessity for uniformity at least to this extent."—(Sargent, *Private Schools.*)

12. Q. What further means are taken by Catholic schools to promote true Americanism?

A. 1. They teach love of country. Love of country, like love of God, is developed in our children by daily instruction and training.

2. They give all due time to the study of American history with the idea of developing in our children admiration and love for the country we call our own.

3. They devote definite periods weekly to the study of civics and the duties and responsibilities of citizenship.

4. They make the English language the medium of instruction and teach our children to love and respect that language and its literature.

5. They observe all the national patriotic holidays with appropriate exercises.

6. They possess and fly an American flag on appropriate days.

7. They welcome the foreign-born or the sons of the foreign-born with a sympathy and love which is truly American, as well as Catholic.

8. Some Catholic schools are centers of Americanization work, where groups of foreign-born meet and are educated along American lines.

13. Q. What is the motto of every Catholic school?

A. The motto of every Catholic school is "For God and Country."

REFERENCES

McClancy, "Americanization and the Catholic Elementary Schools," *Proceedings C. E. A.,* 1919.

Coler, *Socialism in the Schools,* Benziger, N. Y., 1911.

Coler, *Two and Two Make Four,* Beattys & Company, N. Y., 1914.

Williams, *American Catholics in the War,* Macmillan, 1921.

Civics Catechism on the Rights and Duties of American Citizens, N. C. W. C., Washington, D. C., 1919.

Lapp, *The Catholic Citizen,* Macmillan, N. Y., 1921.

CHAPTER XI

Cost of Catholic Education

1. Q. What does it cost yearly to educate a child in the public elementary school?

A. In 1920 the States paid $950,000,000 for the educa-tion of 23,250,000 children in elementary schools, or at the rate of approximately $40 a child. The annual expendi-tures for public education in elementary schools in the United States from 1870 to 1918 are shown in the follow-ing diagram:

DIAGRAM SHOWING ANNUAL EXPENDITURES FOR PUBLIC EDUCATION, 1870-1918.

Burgess, *Trends of School Costs.*

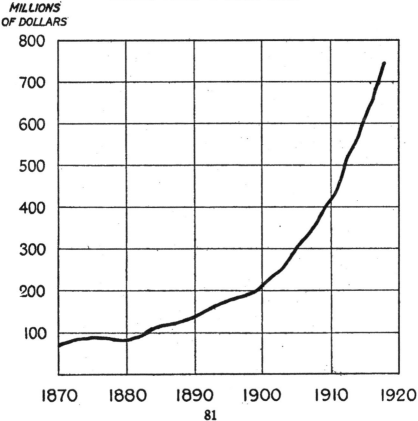

According to the Federal Bureau of Education, in 1918 the expenditure was $763,678,000 for 20,549,000 children. Of this sum $421,084,254, or 52.2 per cent, went for teachers' salaries. This money was distributed as follows:

DIAGRAM SHOWING DISTRIBUTION OF EXPENSE OF PUBLIC SCHOOL EDUCATION.

Burgess, *Trends of School Costs.*

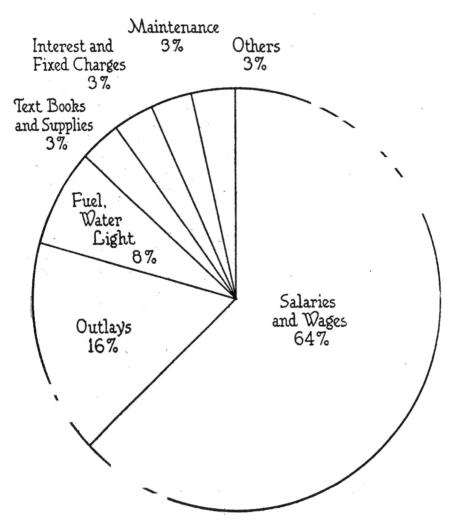

2. Q. What would be the corresponding annual cost to the States for the education of all the children now in Catholic elementary schools?

A. On the basis of $40 per capita, it would amount, exclusive of buildings and equipment, to $71,826,920. This is much more than double what it was estimated to have been in 1910—namely, $30,511,010. To the above must be added the interest at 5 per cent on the value of the ground, buildings and equipment of Catholic elementary schools, estimated at $143,653,840, which is $7,182,692. The total annual saving to the States, therefore, would be $79,009,612.

A more accurate total might be compiled by comparing the cost of public education in the State of Ohio, a state which reflects conditions of both the public schools and the Catholic schools throughout the nation better, than a total based on the cost of public education throughout the United States.

According to the Department of Public Instruction of the State of Ohio, for teaching alone it cost $29.56 per pupil in the elementary schools of that State. In 1920 there were 122,964 children in the Catholic elementary schools of Ohio. It would, therefore, cost the State of Ohio $3,634,815 additional merely for the tuition of their children. If we, therefore, conservatively assume that $30 is a fairly accurate per capita cost for each parish school pupil throughout the United States, the Catholic elementary schools save the nation, in salaries of teachers alone, at least $53,870,190 annually. To this, however, must be added the interest at 5 per cent on the value of the ground, buildings and equipment of Catholic schools, which is $7,182,692.

The total saving to the nation yearly, therefore, would

be, on the very conservative computation of $30 per capita, approximately $61,000,000.

3. Q. What would it cost the State to replace, with new buildings and equipment, Catholic elementary schools?

A. Only a general, estimate can be given. The latest government figures fix the unit classroom cost of new buildings at $12,800. This figure undoubtedly applies to the highest type of urban school. If we, for the basis of an estimate, use one-half of this unit price, or $6,400, as the average unit classroom cost of urban and rural schools, and allow for forty pupils per classroom, it would cost the State, exclusive of school sites, approximately $288,000,000 to provide the Catholic elementary school population with new buildings and equipment. Inasmuch, however, as the Catholic school population is estimated to be 80 per cent urban, this total would be insufficient to replace our schools.

4. Do Catholics actually expend $61,000,000 annually for elementary education?

A. No. Exact statistics as to the average cost of maintenance per pupil in Catholic elementary schools are not available. It is perhaps one-half and certainly one-third the cost of educating a child in the public elementary schools.

5. Q. What is the value of Catholic elementary school buildings and equipment in the United States?

A. No accurate figures are available either as to the actual number of buildings or as to their value. According to Dr. Burns, President of Notre Dame University, in 1912 the "average value of elementary school houses and sites, together with library and all other property, is $71.99 per pupil registered." In 1920 the sum is undoubtedly larger because there has been a very great increase in the cost of materials and wages since 1913.

Eighty dollars per pupil would be a very conservative estimate in 1920 of the average value of Catholic school buildings, sites and equipment.

At $80 per pupil the value would be $143,653,840.

6. Q. What salaries are paid teachers in Catholic elementary schools?

A. No exact records are available of the amount of salary paid Catholic elementary school teachers. It is less than $635, the average of the minimum yearly salary paid to public school teachers. If the Catholic elementary school teachers were paid $635, it would cost the nation $26,403,935 in added salaries for teachers alone.

Catholic elementary school teachers, however, receive much less than what is paid public school teachers.

7. Q. How much does high school education cost?

A. In the public high schools of Ohio it cost $49.30 per capita to educate a pupil. If this average is accepted for the whole country, the Catholic high school system saves the nation approximately $6,401,013 yearly, exclusive of the cost of buildings, equipment, etc.

It has been estimated that in 1917 it cost $14 yearly per girl and $18 yearly per boy to educate Catholic high school pupils. These figures are a most conservative estimate and should certainly be increased to $15 and $20 for 1920. At this rate, Catholics pay annually for high school education the sum of $2,101,080. This figure does not include 6,518 unclassified high school students. The fact that many Catholic high schools, especially for girls, are boarding schools was not taken into consideration in arriving at the above estimate.

8. Q. How much is expended yearly for the education of seminarians?

A. The average annual per capita cost for the education

of a seminarian would be approximately $300. In the large diocesan seminaries it approximates $550. This figure includes board and lodging. At $300, $3,359,400 is expended yearly on the education of candidates for the priesthood.

9. Q. How much is expended yearly for Catholic college education?

A. According to recent figures of the Federal Bureau of Education, the estimated cost in 1918 per capita for college students, including collegiate, preparatory and professional departments, was:

Public Colleges and Universities..................$509.95
Private Colleges and Universities................ 291.31
and the average for public and private, $364.92.

At $291.31 per capita, the cost of educating, exclusive of board and lodging, the students at Catholic colleges in 1920 would be $9,846,895.

No statistics are available from Catholic sources as to the per capita cost of Catholic college education. The average tuition, however, in a Catholic college for men is $100 yearly. At this rate, Catholics expend $2,814,500 annually. For the education of women the average rate of tuition, board included, is $670. At this rate, $7,391,440 is expended yearly. In all, $10,205,940 is spent for college education. These figures do not include 2,927 unclassified college students.

The above sum, however, does not represent more than 50 per cent of what is actually spent, as it does not include interest on the cost of buildings, equipment, etc., nor does it include board and lodging for men students, which items are generally supplied in Catholic colleges. $20,000,000 annually more probably represents the actual sum expended by Catholics on college education.

10. Q. What is the total of money spent yearly by Catholics on Catholic education in the United States?

A. The total annual amount is estimated to be $73,000,-000. This is not an exact total and probably represents but 75 per cent of the actual amount spent every year.

11. Q. Is this not an unwise expenditure on the part of Catholics?

A. Catholics do not estimate the value of their religion in dollars and cents. Since the State schools do not provide an education conformable to Catholic standards, we have no alternative but to spend large sums in training the young according to the dictates of our conscience.

12. Q. Do Catholics pay taxes for the support of public education?

A. They do. Catholics pay their proportionate share for the maintenance of public education besides carrying the financial burden of supporting their own school system. However, it must be remembered that the taxes of Catholics would be much heavier if the cost of educating Catholic children were added to the tax budget.

REFERENCES

Burgess, *Trends of School Costs,* Russell Sage Foundation, N. Y., 1920.

Burns, *Growth and Development of the Catholic School in the United States,* Benziger, N. Y., 1912.

Burns, *Catholic Education,* Longmans, Green & Co., N. Y., 1917.

Statistical Survey of Education, 1917-18, Federal Bureau of Education, Washington, D. C., 1920.

Stevens, *How Much Does Higher Education Cost?* Federal Bureau of Education, Washington, D. C., 1919.

CHAPTER XII

How You Can Help Catholic Education

1. Q. Mention some ways in which you can be of assistance to the cause of Catholic education.

A. You can help Catholic education by sending your children to Catholic schools; by showing your appreciation of the merits of Catholic education; by informing yourself of the aims and purposes of Catholic education; by spreading information about your school; by assisting in its financial support.

2. Q. How do you help Catholic education by sending your children to Catholic schools?

A. Until "every child is in a Catholic school," where this is possible, our educational hopes remain unfulfilled. If you send your children to a Catholic school, your neighbor will probably follow your example.

3. Q. Why should you send your boy or girl to high school and to college?

A. Because higher education opens to the mind the whole field of human thought and endeavor.

Because higher education is necessary for the preparation of leaders, both in civic and in Catholic life.

Because higher education is the only sure preparation for a successful life.

According to a recent compilation, of the 33,000,000 boys and girls who stopped their education after the eighth grade, 808 "became distinguished;" of the 2,000,000 who completed high school, 1,245 "became noted," of the 1,000,000 college graduates, 5,763 "reached distinction." With an elementary school education, therefore, the chances for success are one in 41,250; with a high school education, one in 1,608; with a college education, one in 173.

The following charts from the *Money Value of Education,* by A. Caswell Ellis, published in 1917, represent in dollars and cents what is the value of a high school education:

WHAT FOUR YEARS IN SCHOOL PAID
WAGES OF TWO GROUPS OF BROOKLYN CITIZENS.

	Those Who Left School at 14 (Yearly Salary)	Those Who Left School at 18 (Yearly Salary)
When 14 years of age........	$200	$ ....
When 16 years of age........	250	....
When 18 years of age........	350	500
When 20 years of age........	475	750
When 22 years of age........	575	1,000
When 24 years of age........	600	1,150
When 25 years of age........	688	1,550
Total Salary 11 years........	5,112.50	
Total Salary 7 years.........		$7,337.50

The figures represent the average of actual salaries received by two groups of children that left school at 14 and 18 years of age, respectively, and were investigated by the Committee on Incentives of the Brooklyn Teachers' Association.

SALARIES PAID UNIVERSITY GRADUATES
THE INCOMES RECEIVED FROM THEIR OWN WORK FOR THE FIRST TEN YEARS AFTER LEAVING COLLEGE WERE REPORTED BY GRADUATES AS FOLLOWS:

Graduates of	1st Year	2d Year	3d Year	4th Year	5th Year
Princeton 1901	$706	$ 902	$1,199	$1,651	$2,039
Princeton 1906	860	1,165	1,332	1,427	2,226
Yale 1906	740	969	1,287	1,523	1,887

RECORDS FOR SECOND FIVE YEARS:

Graduates of	6th Year	7th Year	8th Year	9th Year	10th Year
Princeton ..1901	$2,408	$2,382	$2,709	$3,222	$3,804

The figures are from "The Fifth-Year Record of the Class of 1906, Princeton University," pp. 245-259. Reports were from about two-thirds of the members of the classes. In the same way, ten years after graduation, the class of 1899 of Dartmouth reports an average income of $2,097; the class of 1903 of Northwestern University an average of $1,863 for the fifth to tenth year after graduation; and the Harvard Law Class of 1905 reports an average of $2,616 the fifth year after graduating in Law.

4. Q. Why should you send your boy or girl to a Catholic high school and later to a Catholic college?

A. Because the atmosphere is religious, and therefore wholesome.

Because the instructors are religious, and therefore believe what you believe.

Because the training is superior, and therefore better than that given in most State or non-sectarian schools.

Because the adolescent boy and girl need in an especial way the support and safeguards which religion alone gives.

Because the companionship is clean and inspiring, and therefore you need fear no moral contamination for your children.

Because recreation and athletics are kept within reasonable bounds, and therefore not likely to be a hindrance to the acquisition of knowledge.

Because study is supervised, and therefore more apt to be productive of good results.

5. Q. What reasons should impel you to appreciate the work of Catholic education?

A. (a) Catholic education is religious. As you love your religion, so you should love the greatest agency which the Church possesses in America to spread knowledge—the Catholic school.

(b) Catholic education is efficient. Its teachers, its schools and its students prove this efficiency. A study of the Catholic school system impresses one with its manifest superiority. Non-Catholic educators, statesmen, business men appreciate the thoroughness and excellence of Catholic education. We cannot and do not expect less of our Catholic people.

(c) Catholic education is superior education. The Catholic school is the equal and in many cases the superior of any school, either public or private. Catholics should appreciate this fact.

6. Q. Why should you spread information about Catholic schools?

A. Because the Catholic school is not known as it deserves to be known, even among Catholics. The statistics of the Catholic school system, the training of its teachers, the patriotic purposes of its existence, should be made known to all. You cannot expect appreciation of your schools, especially by outsiders, unless you make known in conversation and by writing the facts about Catholic schools.

The development of Catholic education in the United States, particularly during the last hundred years, has been little short of miraculous. The mere existence of thousands of Catholic schools with an approximate attendance of two million, should be enough to convince any man that Catholicism in the United States is alive to its duties and conscious of its divine purposes as the greatest religious force in the Republic.

Never lose an opportunity, therefore, of speaking about your schools or of urging on all a fair study and evaluation of the same.

7. Q. Is there a Catholic rural problem in education?

A. Yes. The farms of this country are being depopulated by large migrations to the city. It is estimated that 80 per cent of the Catholic population is urban, 20 per cent rural. This rural percentage is decreasing every year. Of Catholic school attendance, it is estimated that 90 per cent is urban and 10 per cent rural. Thousands of children, therefore, who live in the country are not receiving a Catholic education. Coupled with this loss in numbers is the loss in leadership, both civic and religious. It is a well known fact that a large percentage of the noted men and women of America have been farm boys and girls, while in Europe a high percentage of religious vocations comes from the smaller towns and the country.

8. Q. What can we do to help solve Catholic rural problems in education?

A. (a) We must, first of all, be convinced of the fact that there is a Catholic rural problem and that it is in the interest of the Church to help solve it.

(b) Rural religious leadership must be developed and the rural Catholic school must be considered as important as the city parish school.

(c) Catholic vacation schools should be founded in those districts where the Catholic population is too small to maintain a rural parish school.

(d) The formation of groups of lay catechists, who would go to places where there is no church or school and regularly teach religion.

(e) The development of a correspondence course in rural religious education, which should be of such a character as to reach every Catholic who lives on a farm.

9. Q. Why should you assist your schools financially?

A. Because financial assistance is a moral duty. Not only does the Church command you to support your schools, but conscience should convince you that you must do so.

No Catholic should require urging to support Catholic education. He should do it willingly because of the necessity of Christian education, because of its admitted efficiency, because it is thoroughly American, and because of his loyalty to the Church.

10. Q. Do Protestant denominations support their schools?

A. In 1921, ten Protestant organizations asked for $240,-000,000 for their educational institutions. The Methodists alone sought $22,940,000. Most of this money will be devoted to higher education.

11. Q. How much money would the Catholic Church require to make its educational institutions secure?

A. An eminent Catholic educator has estimated that a trust fund of $50,000,000 would provide for the current needs of Catholic higher education, and another $50,000,000 would probably be required for Catholic elementary education.

12. Q. How can you assist Catholic education financially?

A. In many ways:

(a) By contributing your share to the upkeep of your parish school. The burden of Catholic education must be borne by each and every individual.

(b) By setting aside in your will a definite sum of money for educational purposes. No loyal Catholic should make a will without making provisions for the education of his own children and for the support of Catholic education.

(c) By endowing Catholic colleges and schools. All colleges have endowment funds; you may be able to endow a professorship or even a class-room.

(d) By providing scholarships for worthy boys and girls. Many scholarships in our colleges have been founded by individuals. In some places, groups of men and women have organized to give scholarships to ambitious boys and girls who desire a college education. No greater service, either to the Church or to our young people, could be performed by any community.

(e) By assisting young men in their education for the holy priesthood and by helping to build and endow seminaries.

(f) By supporting the efforts now being made to train Catholic men and women as social workers. In this respect, the National Catholic Service School for Women deserves universal support.

(g) By supplying our parish schools with adequate playgrounds and playground equipment, library facilities, and schoolroom necessities.

(h) By encouraging the efforts now being made to establish Catholic vacation summer camps for boys and girls.

(i) By supplying the funds with which Catholic education can be given to those who live in the country and cannot attend city parish schools. The Catholic education of children whose parents are farmers is one of the most serious problems which the Church faces today.

References

What Women's Organizations Can Do, National Council Catholic Women, Washington, D. C., 1921.

O'Hara, *The Rural Problem in Its Bearings on Catholic Education,* Catholic Educational Association, 1921.

Ellis, *The Money Value of Education,* Federal Bureau of Education, Washington, D. C., 1917.

LIST OF TABLES AND CHARTS

INDEX

97

Lightning Source UK Ltd.
Milton Keynes UK
UKHW021040110119
335297UK00012B/1697/P

—